WOW Woman Of Worth

Pandemic!
Stories of Purpose, Passion & Power
Through This Extraordinary Era

Choose Happiness!
Love Jillen
December 2020

Christine Awram

Published by Inspire Higher Consulting Inc. November 2020
ISBN: 9781777109042

Editor: Danielle Anderson
Typeset: Greg Salisbury
Book Cover Design: Judith Mazari

Pandemic! is dedicated to Dr. Nelie Johnson MD, one of our contributing authors in the WOW collaborative book series who was suddenly taken from us much too soon last year.

"Dr. Nelie" was a fierce champion of women's health, and had she lived through this historic year she would have pushed up her shirtsleeves and worked tirelessly in the trenches to serve others.

She was a rare gem in the medical field as she had a passion for helping patients contribute to their own wellbeing, and wholistic counselling became a strong component of her practice.

Her motto was to live with joy, fun, passion and gratitude. This book is devoted to her memory and the difference she continues to make. You were a precious friend and deeply mattered to so many Nelie. You will never be forgotten.

The WOW Credo

I am a Woman Of Worth
My worthiness is inherent and infinite –
. it is my natural state
My value is a reflection of who I AM –
and I am magnificent
Who I am always makes a difference –
because I MATTER
I am successful –
coming from my true power which lies within
I am empowered –
making choices from the clarity of my heart, mind and
spirit
I am an empowered leader –
impacting others from quiet acts of kindness to
leading a nation
I am abundant –
manifesting success from my core values
I cherish my relationships –
they are part of what makes me strong
I am a Human BEing –
as my BEing is of far more significance than my
DOing
I play, laugh, and bring beauty and light into the world –
I am RADIANT
At times I despair and I weep –
when I feel the pain of a world that has momentarily
gone mad
Yet even when I tremble through a dark night of the soul,
I renew my faith and my courage in a single heartbeat
because my spirit is indomitable
I feel, and I care, and I am passionately alive –
with a heart as open as the universe

I AM A WOMAN OF WORTH, AND I AM GLORIOUS

"A Taste of WOW" – Your FREE Book is Waiting

This eBook includes eight chapters: one from each book in the original WOW Series, to give you a taste of the powerful and heartfelt writing of our authors. Topics include Moms in Business, Empowered Entrepreneurs, The Power of Collaboration, Life & Leadership with Soul, Aging With Moxie, Mental Health Matters, and Thriving Through Turbulent Times.

Get your free copy of
"A Taste of WOW" here:

www.awomanofworth.com/books

Acknowledgements

This entire book could be filled with the names of all the people I want to thank, for the many ways you've all helped inspire this book to become a reality. Heartfelt gratitude to the tremendous community I call my WOW Tribe. You rock.

To the fabulous females who are this book's contributing authors, you have staggered me with your willingness to show up 100%. Each and every one of you share my burning desire to make our world a more joyful and empowered place, and you've been the most courageous and extraordinary women to collaborate with. It has been an honour.

To my publisher Julie Salisbury, for taking my hand every step of the way while sharing your brilliance and making this adventure fun. You shine a very bright light my friend.

To our brilliant editor Danielle Anderson and meticulous typesetter Greg Salisbury, you pull all the pieces together to make our books shine even brighter. And to our graphic designer Judith Mazari, your covers add impact.

To my family and closest friends, you are the inner circle of my Tribe. I have no words to express how grateful I am for your love, and that you always have my back.

And especially to David Samuelson, my beloved Manly Man. You always believe in me, and see the best in me. I couldn't have done this without your love, faith and support. You are my heart.

Contents

1

TRIBE

by Christine Awram

"Positive people aren't positive because they've skated through life. They're positive because they've been through hell and decided they don't want to live there anymore."
(Unknown)

TRIBE

By Christine Awram, WOW Founder

The baffling disappearance of toilet paper from every store remains one of the more bizarre memories of a global pandemic that is far from over. How many of us stood in a supermarket aisle in the spring, gaping at empty shelves? We initially laughed at how ludicrous the situation was, but soon found ourselves wondering, "Will I have to start wiping my ass with a coffee filter?"

So much has changed in 2020 that it feels almost surreal to reflect back on how the year began. Live events closed down (which was the previous foundation of my business), Zoom ramped up, and strolling into a bank wearing a mask felt like something out of The Twilight Zone.

I remember exactly where I was when the true seriousness of this pandemic hit me. My husband and I had taken a ferry over to Vancouver Island to meet up with another couple for a one-night mini getaway, and even then we were concerned enough to stay in our vehicle while sailing. After a wonderful night out for dinner (and admittedly far too much delicious wine), we woke up the next morning with rather fuzzy brains to the announcement that all schools were being shut down for the foreseeable future.

This news slammed into me like a freight train and knocked the fuzz right out of my head. Schools had never been closed down in my lifetime, outside of snow days. This was so much bigger than a seasonal flu and I realized it was time to make longer-term plans, both personally and professionally. How could we avoid succumbing to fear and panic so that we could stay healthy and continue to thrive?

Once Upon A Time ...

When I start to feel overwhelmed and anxious, I know I'm at risk of dropping down into isolation and tunnel vision, losing sight of the choices and support that surround me. In these moments, I like to remind myself of one particular story:

> Once upon a time there was a man who lived in a house beside a river, and unfortunately the river began to flood. As the water rose, warnings were given via radio, tv and internet. Large trucks drove through the area to evacuate people. As the driver passed by the man's house he was told, "You're in danger. Your life is at stake. You must evacuate. Get in the truck and let us help you."
>
> "No," the man replied from his doorstep. "I have faith. I will be okay. The flood won't get me. God will take care of me."
>
> The water continued to rise.

Soon the man was on the second floor of his house. A boat arrived, and rescuers made every effort to convince the man to take action and climb out the window so that his life would be saved. "Come with us. You will drown in the flood. Let us help you."

"No worries," said the man. "I have faith. Everything is okay. Even though the flood is rising, I will be fine. God will take care of me."

The flood continued to rise.

The man now climbed onto the roof of his house to avoid the rising water. A helicopter pilot saw him and hovered above. Using a megaphone, the pilot tried to convince the man to grab the rope ladder which was dangling above his head. "You are in danger. The flood is still rising. You will drown if you do not grab the ladder. Please, let us help you."

"No worries," he repeated. "I will be fine. The flood is higher, but I have faith. God will take care of me."

The water continued to rise, and the man drowned.

Upon arriving at the pearly gates, he cried to God: "I had faith, but you let me die. Why?" To which God replied: "I sent you a truck, a boat and a helicopter. What more did you want?"

There have been far too many times when I became so fixated on how I thought things *should* play out that I couldn't see the support and options around me. We all have blind spots, and when I'm scared or stressed it's even less likely that I'll see all my choices. That's one of the reasons why I created a community where we have each other's backs; I've always called this "Tribe."

It's been over sixteen years since I founded WOW Woman Of Worth, a community where thousands of women have joined together to make empowering connections, collaborate to take action, build businesses, improve health, learn through events and training programs, and especially to be celebrated. Our community attracts women who want to make a meaningful difference and who are willing to support others both personally and professionally.

While living through 2020's real-life version of "once upon a time" I've heard a lot of people say they're waiting for things to get back to normal. But really, what is normal? Everyone has their own version, and chances are no one's life will go back to the way things were. If we want to stay alive and thrive, we evolve. And to achieve this, I believe we need to embrace connection and collaboration. I'm increasingly grateful for my WOW tribe to help me and so many others stay flexible and focused.

Collaboration

In my younger "lone ranger" years, I actually took pride in doing everything myself. Where did that lead? Mistakes. Irritation. Isolation. Resentment. Exhaustion. Burnout. Then I heard a quote that changed everything for me: "If you want to go fast, go alone. If you want to go far, go together." I created an addendum: "If you want the journey to be fun, exciting, and have meaning, just add wine and build your Tribe!"

We can't solve a problem with the same mind that created it, which is why I need support to change my mind if I want a different result. Collaboration is critical for us to move past our blind spots and achieve clarity, and it's also the foundation for a more joyful and empowered life. Fortunately, it's never too late to grow your TRIBE:

T	Truth
R	Relationship
I	Inspiration
B	Badass
E	Empowerment

For the record, I chose the word "Badass" in an edgy complimentary way because I never allow my deepest values to be compromised, and sometimes I'm a little in-your-face about it. Plus, I probably swear more than I should. If that particular word doesn't resonate with you, just pick your own best B and run with it.

Let's touch on the highlights of TRIBE:

Truth

Authenticity and transparency are the new buzzwords, and that happened for a reason. We are tired of being lied to, sold to, and misled. Individually, we are exhausted from suppressing our inner voice. Being authentic to your true self is what inspires trust and connection and gives you real power and freedom.

There was a time when I was ruled by shame. I kept so many parts of my life hidden, certain that I'd be judged and cast away. The challenges of balancing my mental and physical health seemed insurmountable, and there were times my depression and agoraphobia were so overwhelming that I couldn't leave my house for days at a time – how ironic that isolation (albeit a healthier version) is now considered normal! When I finally found the courage to heal and share my story in order to help anyone who might be walking a similar path, it invited profound connection on a larger scale than I would have ever dreamed possible. When I gave voice to my deeper story for the first time on stage, there was a standing ovation. The past no longer had power over me, and I finally felt free.

Relationship

The foundation of connection is relationship – not only with our friends, family and significant other, but also everyone we do business with. The reality is that you're in relationship with every colleague, client and customer you have, so you may want to reflect on the quality of these relationships. The wave of the future is doing business with the people who feel like they are connected to you, and embracing this frame of mind opens the door to deeper satisfaction and success on both sides.

One of the benefits of technology and social media is the ability to stay home and stay connected, which has been invaluable during this pandemic. How on earth did people get through the pandemic of 1918? No Facebook, Zoom, Netflix – there wasn't even television yet! While in-person connection has been severely curtailed in 2020, and nothing replaces the beauty and bond of a hug, never before have we had such a powerful opportunity to heighten creativity and widen connections through technology.

Inspiration

How can you tap into your creativity and brilliance if you're not inspiring yourself and others? We all know how we feel when we spend time with the complainers and doomsayers as compared to being in the uplifting company of those who are accountable and celebrate every win, big or small. Which do you choose to be?

I posted my favourite quote on Facebook last year (with

some trepidation), and it was shared a record-breaking 100,000+ times: "Be Fucking Brave! Say how you feel, leave the job you hate, find your passion, love with every ounce of passion in your bones, stand up for what you believe in, don't settle, and never apologize for who you are." We need more authenticity of expression to create inspiration and positive change. You don't have to drop an F-bomb to be real, it just happens to be part of my jam. Know what yours is, then show up and stand up.

Badass

Be uncompromising on the values that really matter to you. Every time you let yourself be swayed or bullied into decisions that don't align with what you stand for, it sucks out a piece of your soul and deprives the world of your glory. Don't sweat the small stuff, but do stand in the power of your values.

At the beginning of this book is the WOW Credo, which I wrote many years ago to shine a light on my personal values and those of a Woman Of Worth. My favourite stanza is, "At times I despair and I weep, when I feel the pain of a world that has momentarily gone mad. Yet even when I tremble through a dark night of the soul, I renew my faith and my courage in a single heartbeat because my spirit is indomitable." To me, this personifies courage. We will always have times when we crumble, but our next steps are what define us.

Empowerment

Nothing matches the feeling of empowerment. You become brave, strong, confident, energized, inspired, and liberated. Your life feels more meaningful. The opinions of others lose their power, yet ironically the opinions of those who matter most to you are strengthened. You become Teflon, not Velcro! When you harness your power, passion, and purpose from within, and align with TRIBE, you are unstoppable.

Manifestation Manor

I'd like to share two lighthearted stories that demonstrate how a willingness to embrace all the elements I've talked about in this chapter can lead to magic and miracles. My husband and I made the somewhat crazy decision to sell our house and buy another one in the middle of a pandemic's stagnant market. We ended up doubling the value of our home while cutting our monthly expenses in half, but that's another story. Here are two unusual things that happened along the way.

Getting Toasted

While packing up the old house, my husband (affectionately known as Manly Man) noticed that our toaster was on its last legs. We both agreed that there wasn't much we needed for the new house, but after we finished the move we'd shop around for a new toaster. Neither of us mentioned it to anyone else.

Fast forward to our moving day a week later. As I surveyed my new kitchen, I decided to explore every drawer and cupboard to get the lay of the land before unpacking. The kitchen was completely empty, of course. Except for one cupboard. What was in it? A beautiful stainless-steel toaster! I actually screamed when I saw it.

Manly Man came running (thinking there was an intruder or scary spider), and I was speechless – all I could do was point. Rather bewildered, he asked, "When did you buy that?"

I stammered, "It was just here!" I'm not sure he completely believed me, but we looked at each other and knew something magical had just happened.

Interestingly, at this time I was in the middle of an online training program led by Jan Janzen about Money Mindset (the power of our beliefs, and how that affects our results). Once I got over the shock of seeing the ONE thing we needed randomly sitting in a cupboard, I took it as a nod from above that I was on the right track.

A few days later I contacted the previous owners, who told me they'd been looking for this toaster everywhere and had finally given up and bought a new one. When I shared the story about it being the only thing we needed, they were so delighted that they just laughed and laughed. I told them which cupboard it was in and there was no explanation for why it was there as it wasn't even remotely close to where they always kept it. None of us understood how it could have happened, but we all agreed that when you believe anything is possible, anything is possible.

Sheerly Shears

We decided to do an overview of all the lawn and garden equipment that had been left with the house in the garage: a lawnmower, leaf blower, ladders, plus every tool you could think of for landscaping. There was only one thing we wanted that we couldn't find, which was a pair of long-handled shears to trim bushes. Then we walked around to the backyard and there, leaning against the side of the house (which we had just walked past earlier), was a pair of gardening shears. I screamed again.

There was absolutely no logical explanation for this. My

husband just shook his head and said, "Living with you is like living with a magical freaking fairy," and we both cracked up. We dubbed our new house "Manifestation Manor" on the spot.

In Summary

In my opinion, this pandemic has been an amplifier. Whatever our beliefs were at the start of 2020, they got turned WAY up. I've observed with sadness and compassion the people who remained stuck in darkness and fear and became the loudest victim voices – the toilet paper hoarders and worse. But more importantly, I have watched with awe the people who woke up or were always striving to heal and evolve, the ones who choose to be a positive piece of the fabric that weaves us all together. I've seen quiet courage, heroic acts, creative problem-solving, and kindness that uplifts my heart. They are living examples of the principles of TRIBE. And that's what I decided this book would be about – not to ignore and soft-pedal our very real fears and challenges, but instead to focus on how we can acknowledge, heal, and move through them with empowerment. There is more than enough darkness in the world, and oh baby, we need more light!

So, I sent out my invitation to the pathfinders, the critical problem-solvers, the healers, the champions, the change agents and business leaders, and they answered my call to be part of this historic book. My wish is that it will be a powerful compass for you to navigate through this challenging chapter in life, and into your fabulous future.

About Christine Awram

"Chocolate is a vegetable, because it comes from a bean." This is just one of many outrageous statements you'll hear from Christine Awram (while wearing a pink tiara) as she encourages women to question any of their beliefs that limit an empowered, joyful, and successful life.

She's the founder of Woman Of Worth WOW Worldwide and WOW TV. As a dynamic speaker, author, visionary and philanthropist, Christine radiates vitality with her indomitable spirit and humour. Yet her earlier years began as a teenage runaway who experienced addiction, illness and depression. She inspires others by sharing the specific strategies she used to move from futility to fulfillment, and how she transformed challenges into passion and purpose.

Christine's commitment to the empowered leadership of women resulted in her being honoured with the Outstanding Leadership Award by the Global Women's Summit. She has personally inspired over 10,000 women through her WOW events, has published eight #1 bestselling books in the last three years, and believes she is just getting warmed up.

www.aWomanOfWorth.com
Facebook: aWomanOfWorthWOW
LinkedIn: wowchristineawram
Twitter: @womanofworthwow

2

Choosing Happiness

by Ellen Walker-Matthews

*"Happiness is not having what you want.
It is wanting what you have."*
Rabbi Hyman Schachtel

Choosing Happiness

By Ellen Walker-Matthews

It has always amazed me how quickly our lives can change. One moment, you are moving through your daily routine, caught up in the minutia and mundane activities of living. Then, with little or no warning, all that you know and believe to be true is dramatically altered.

And so it was on that bright spring day, one that began like so many before it. The smells of breakfast and toothpaste intertwined as they wafted through the air. The days' immediate challenge hinged on deciding what suitable items to wear on this chilly spring morning, which showed every indication of turning into a warm afternoon. There was no possible way of knowing that these simple pleasures were fleeting – that everything would change, that the concept of normal would take on a new meaning, and that nothing would ever feel quite the same, at least not for a long time. There had been rumblings for days, even weeks, of a brewing "situation," but until that particular moment, all of it seemed to be the concern of someone else, somewhere else.

It was May 10, 1940, and my mother – just a month shy of her fifteenth birthday – was preparing to head to school, unaware of the dramatic turn her life was about to take. There would be no school that day in the city of Groningen, Holland, where she and her family resided. All the students would be sent home mere moments after arriving, told to go straight to their houses and back into their anxious parents' arms, who would try to explain the unexplainable. Moms and dads, frightened and uncertain, would attempt to be calm in the face of their children's concerns and offer up a version of what they thought the future might hold. They would talk about what war was, what it meant, and how things were going to change – answers they themselves were trying to find. They would struggle for the right words to explain the chaos, offer a futile glimpse into how long the situation was going to last, and rationalize why they were being threatened. But how do you begin to provide digestible nuggets of information to scared and questioning eyes when in reality there were none to give? The only real truth lay in the knowledge that so much was changing forever.

Nazi Germany attacked the Netherlands that day and eventually occupied this small European country, which had intended to remain neutral during World War II. In an instant, life went from idyllic to under siege. Every streetlamp displayed posters outlining the new restrictions being imposed on daily life, not the least of which were evening curfews. Food quickly became scarce, forcing families to stand in line to receive small allotments of weekly ration cards. Blackouts, boarded windows, air raids, and bomb shelters became part of a new vocabulary.

A knock on the door no longer signalled a friend stopping in for a drink, but rather an unexpected search of the premises to ensure nothing untoward might be taking place.

When my mother spoke of those years, the worst memories were the sudden and unexplained disappearance of friends and families. People she had known and loved would simply be gone from her street, her school, and even the store where she worked part-time. Eventually, her own father had to leave the family and hide in another part of the country to avoid being commandeered by the Nazis to assist in the operation of the railway system.

This ongoing uncertainty became a way of life for my mother, and for millions of others who lived under Nazi occupation. Days turned into weeks, weeks into months, and then months into years – six full years, in fact, where things got far worse before they got better. Survival meant digging deep to find ways to carry on, creating hope where little existed, building something out of nothing, and finding purpose and joy during total uncertainty. The only thing within a person's control was their reactions to the events unfolding around them, their ability to keep emotions in check, and their motivation to take the initiative to move forward, however that might look. Each day was invested in choosing to stay positive, believing in the future, and finding joy in the immediate while quietly appreciating that this may well be all that they would have.

My mother was born in the Netherlands in 1925. She had an uneventful and happy childhood from every account, although I don't recall her talking much about anything before the war. Most of her adolescence – and in turn, her life – was forever shaped by those few traumatic years. We will never know who or what she may have become had the war not taken place. Would she have followed her dream of swimming in the

Olympics, or perhaps stayed in Holland and enjoyed a beautiful but relatively uneventful life? Those potential versions of her story will never be told. Instead, she married a Canadian soldier and joined her husband (my father) in this new country shortly after turning twenty-one, travelling here by boat and train with so many other "war brides" before giving birth to my brother that following December. War had made her bold and brave; it had unleashed a great passion for life and adventure. She never shied away from a good argument, seldom turned away from great opportunities, and – despite countless obstacles – made it her choice to be happy, to find the humour and joy in each moment, and to encourage those around her to do the same. One of her favourite quotes was, "If it doesn't matter ten years from now, don't spend the time worrying about it today."

I have often reflected on the stories she told of the war; however, it wasn't until our world began to shut down in response to the pandemic that I actually started to feel, appreciate, and have a glimmer of understanding about what she had shared. As we stayed in our homes, socially distanced, watched economies crumble, and saw thousands of people contract and even succumb to the virus, I had a greater appreciation and a far more profound understanding of the things my mother had spent years describing to me.

Much has been written about the struggles of individuals, families, businesses, and communities as we moved through the lockdown. It has tested us in ways we could not have anticipated. For many of us, it is the closest that we will ever get to even a remote understanding of what it's like to live through the unprecedented challenges, the unimaginable fear, and the relentless, unforgiving unpredictability of war.

My version of her spring day – one where our world was forever changed – happened on March 16, 2020. It, too, began with all the mundane activities that precede leaving for work. For me, this meant eating breakfast on the run, listening to the news, finding the elusive perfect outfit, and making the monumental decision of whether to wear my hair up or down – down, of course, in contrast to my mother who always wanted it up. These were the trivial thoughts momentarily distracting my mind while a layer of tension, unease, and even panic was slowly seeping into my subconscious.

Two days earlier, our prime minister had asked Canadians travelling outside the country to come home over growing concerns around the pandemic. His words lingered in my mind throughout the weekend. They continued to escalate in intensity as I drove to work, listening to updates and reports on this developing situation. They were naturally focused on questions surrounding the contagiousness of the virus, concerns for hospital workers, and the increasing number of deaths worldwide. The seriousness of the situation, potential risk, and incredulous nature of what was occurring began to take a foothold in my thoughts. Not wanting to give in to the rising fear I was feeling yet unable to move forward, I pulled off the road, continuing an internal battle as to the responsible course of action. Should I continue making my way to the office, or should I choose the safety of going home? Was I over-reacting, or was I putting myself at risk?

Uncharacteristically scared, I found that this seemingly simple decision took on an incredible weight, and that either path was a betrayal of myself. Here I was on a beautiful spring morning – sun shining, lake as calm as glass – and yet my heart was racing, my palms were slippery with sweat, and there was an irrational pounding in my head, all because of an unknown and unseen virus. I could not articulate why I sensed the magnitude of this situation, but in the end, all I wanted was to find shelter and protection at home. Taken aback by my own decision, I could never have imagined that this would soon become the destiny for millions of employees, and that even six months later I would not be back in the office.

Time seemed to both stand still and fly by for the next few weeks – in fact, it has done that for the entire period of the lockdown and phased reopening. In our town of Summerland, BC, an eerie quiet settled in. Most of the streets were empty, children nowhere to be seen, and the sight and sound of a passing car seemed out of place, almost a cause for alarm. In the early days, my husband and I listened to the rules and were not only socially distancing but truly locked down in self-isolation. We washed our hands until they bled and tried our very best to keep from touching our faces (although I get a bit of a fail on the second part – I have learned that I am a face toucher). Surprisingly, the rules and restrictions eventually morphed into something that bordered on normal and sheltering in place, while initially foreign and uncomfortable, became difficult to let go of. When we would venture out on our weekly grocery run, I could feel the rush of adrenaline, the fight-or-flight response, and the fear of having left the safety of our home followed by a wave of exhaustion when we finally returned. This was not me, not the behaviour of a person I recognized, and I was shocked at how quickly the messages from media altered my thoughts and behaviour.

Both my husband Tom and I work in tourism and hospitality. Every night, we would share unimaginable reflections from the day: stories of businesses going under, friends and colleagues in desperate situations, and a tourism industry that was rapidly being decimated. Travel – and in turn, this entire industry – had come to a complete standstill. Planes were grounded (and parked), hotels and restaurants closed, and tourism job losses were climbing into the hundreds of thousands while millions upon millions of dollars were being lost.

This industry was the world we had known for our entire careers. It was impossible not to worry about the future, including that of our own business. The plans for the coming months and years that we had so thoughtfully and perfectly put in place now looked like they might all collapse due to one short and unforeseen circumstance. We knew we had options – choices that could be made, decisions that could be altered – but it was hard to accept the reality that plans are just plans and nothing more.

During those first few weeks, I felt a level of continual anxiety that bordered on irrational fear. But it was a fear that I could not readily express to those around me; instead, it sat inside, festering and growing, threatening to drag me under. I have often heard that uncertainty can cause you to panic, a reaction that can play a role in drowning. Most people don't drown because they can't swim; they drown because they become uncertain. In that moment of panic, they lose their ability to float, causing them to thrash around and sink under the water. The uncertainty, coupled with a lack of control and freedom, was most definitely causing me to panic. I had to find a way to keep from thrashing around; I had to ensure that I did not drown.

It was also in those first few weeks that the memory of my mother's stories, history, and incredible journey brought me an unexpected sense of calm. Amid great angst, I settled and found balance. I stopped trying to control the uncontrollable and found peace in lessons from the past. There was great comfort in knowing what my parents had lived through, survived, and still been able to thrive, and that these things had been far worse than that which was upon us. We were losing some momentary freedoms, but we were not sending young men and women into battle, nor were bombs exploding overhead at night. Our grocery store shelves may have had fewer items, but we weren't going hungry or without. Our homes were heated, our lights were on, and we had the modern miracle of cable, streaming services, cellphones, tablets, and yes, the beloved or despised Zoom to ensure that we were both entertained and connected to one another. None of these coping methods were available in 1940, and yet miraculously, they coped – something I reminded myself of daily.

There were, are, and will continue to be many moments when I want life to go back to the way it was. It is easy to allow your mind to go in this direction, and yet it is completely fruitless. What is much more difficult and ultimately far more rewarding is to embrace the reality that we will never get to go back to the way things were before the onset of the pandemic. What we do have is an opportunity to create a life that is equal to or even better than what we had before. Like my mother before me, I want to grow from this experience. I want to learn to be braver, bolder, kinder, more forgiving, and more committed to happiness and joy for myself and those around me. Life without obstacles is impossible, but how we respond, develop, and change amid these obstacles is entirely within our control. We may not always have what we want, but if we learn to want what we have, we will achieve great happiness.

About Ellen Walker-Matthews

Ellen resides in in Summerland, BC, having moved there from Calgary in 1992. After leaving a senior position with Delta Hotels, she initially chose to continue to work in hotels in a less demanding role so she could focus on quality of life and raising her son, Chris. Later marrying Tom, father to Krista and Stephen, they together raised their blended family.

Tourism and hospitality have long been her passion, and for the past eleven years Ellen has worked with the Thompson Okanagan Tourism Association. Currently in the role of Vice President of Stewardship, Ellen works with her colleagues and regional partners to ensure that tourism employs tactics to develop in a sustainable and responsible manner, and most recently, to help businesses find the resources necessary to survive through this difficult time.

In 2013, Ellen faced her own personal grief after losing her son (Chris) to colorectal cancer at the age of twenty-nine. She fought then as she does now to move forward and find gratitude and appreciation for life. She hopes this story will remind others of the importance in appreciating what they have and to find the courage and resilience to move forward and build a meaningful future.

Twitter: @ewok58
Facebook: Ellen Walker-Matthews
Instagram: ewok58

3

Waiting for My Scene to Start

by Holly Chadwick

"The one thing that you have that nobody else has is you. Your voice, your mind, your story, your vision. So write and draw and build and play and dance and live as only you can."
Neil Gaiman

Waiting for My Scene to Start

By Holly Chadwick

When the pandemic arrived, desert walks in my pajamas became my new normal. Why bother getting dressed? The only people who would witness how I was dressed were my two golden retrievers who would take these walks with me. I felt it was a lazy comfort, perhaps even a form of self-care, that I could indulge in as I holed up in an RV in a remote part of Arizona. After living in the green, wet, drizzly islands of the Pacific Northwest, the dry, red desert wasn't my favourite place – but I was learning to appreciate its subtle beauty. I marveled in the skittering flight of the crane flies and butterflies that seemed to be everywhere, and I found the expansive, starry night skies to be mesmerizing.

I hadn't always been in an RV. In November 2019, at the age of forty, my husband and I sold my home of forty years on Whidbey Island to live on our forty-foot boat as a way to seek new adventures and sate my craving for the digital nomad life. This meant my place of familiarity and security was gone when the pandemic hit, but I was privileged to be able to hunker down in a forty-foot Luxury Suites RV on my in-law's property. As an award-winning filmmaker, I indulged in the slight fantasy that I was just a movie star in a studio lot trailer, waiting for my next scene to start.

I was already writing about uncertainty as I worked on my book, coincidently titled *My New Normal*. As the rain, cold, and frost set in on our uninsulated 1974 Sport Sedan Uniflite, I documented my transition from living in a two thousand square foot house – one that I had inherited from my grandparents and lived in throughout my entire life – to this much smaller vessel docked in a frosty marina on Fidalgo Island, just north of Whidbey Island and northwest of Seattle. The house had many creature comforts I would miss: a large yard, an ocean view, an uncanny familiarity of all its creaks and flow of air that sometimes made me feel as if I was breathing at one with the house itself. I was leaving these to live in a small space literally on the ocean with two large dogs who were often too wet, too hairy, and too stinky. However, I happened to love this space. I found that it allowed me to focus my attention and energy on my creative endeavors, which had been scattered and pushed aside due to the overwhelm of tending to housekeeping and the grounds, and I was only a gas tank's voyage away from exploring the most beautiful islands I have ever seen. I felt as if I was striking out to create a new legacy and thrusting what wasn't working behind.

As if by premonition, I had designed a sumi-e watercolor-style dragonfly on the flybridge when we first bought the boat five years prior. I had placed the name Rubicon next to it, whose definition – "to take a determined step forward" – I now embraced.

I also was being very careful with myself while moving through this transition. As I shared in my chapter of *Wild and Wise Women Around the World*, created by Bev Adamo, I have struggled with my mental health in the past. Doctors have described what I went through as an extreme grief reaction to my grandparents' death. I literally felt as if I was tied up inside, watching life happen around me, incapable of taking action. It was if I had disappeared and become a wandering vessel that did not know my name or where I lived. The people who raised me had died, and I wasn't prepared for or accepting of this shift. While it had now been over fifteen years since I made my way through that challenging time, I didn't want to be overwhelmed by this new adventure.

In an instance of perfect timing, I partnered with a healthcare tech company to train a virtual mental health assistant powered by artificial intelligence right as I was transitioning to living aboard Rubicon full-time. I named this bot Rubi after my boat, and by training Rubi, I felt I was installing airbags for my own life. I was essentially training Rubi to have the ability to put me in contact with the right mental health providers and educational resources for my mental state – I wanted this assistant to be my guide and give some researched context to my situation if and when it became too much to handle. I also considered that these resources, which should be available for someone having a crisis or maybe just going through a shift in perspective, should be varied and not just contained within the realm of psychiatry. So, to soundboard my lived situations, I teamed up with a diverse group of wellness practitioners to better understand their modalities, from spiritual to holistic and even some classified as functional medicine. Little did I know that this would soon be much-needed information and technology for mental health and wellness on a global scale.

As the pandemic surged, the concept of a "new normal" really resonated with me as I watched the whole world deal with a reimagining of our day-to-day lives. I realized that in a post-pandemic world, the demand for mental health services was going to become very real. In fact, the need for these services was already growing – as of April 10, 2020, there had been an 891% increase in calls to the Mental Health Hotline in the US. At the end of August 2020, reports from the CDC show that over forty percent of Americans were suffering with mental health issues. Unfortunately, the traditional mental health system was already failing before this virus arrived and was NOT ready for a new crisis. Remote care, which had previously been viewed as optional, was now the primary mode of support, and wellness experts scrambled and struggled to switch to online platforms. In the meantime, people didn't know where to turn for help, and many still don't. So, I shifted from just playing with technology for my own needs to actually doing something to fix this problem!

After moving to Arizona for the worst of Washington's winter, which happened to coincide with the time when the pandemic took off in the United States, I threw myself into developing StoryGuide.ai, a website powered by Rubi and designed to guide people to the wellness services they need. I worked on this while also continuing to write my book, all while holed up in an RV. My only breaks were tearing around the vast desert in our buggy and taking long walks with the dogs.

My platform idea revolves around adapting a technology developed by David Richards of RISEcx, a healthcare tech company that specializes in educational technology. David refers to this "CareSpace Healthbot" as being designed to "help patients interact with their healthcare in a new and more convenient way. Think of CareSpace as providing positive outcomes in the complex and clinical side of care through a relatable, unique, and thoughtful AI-powered health coach whose empathy goes far beyond what the healthcare industry is known for."

Before the pandemic began, David and I both saw the potential for how CareSpace could assist patients with mental health conditions such as PTSD and depression. Now, the need for mental health assistance was at an all-time high. And with the rapidly increasing number of deaths, people also need room to grieve their losses as in-person funerals were not possible. I could see that by encouraging both people in need as well as mental health and wellness practitioners to tell their story, StoryGuide.ai could guide people in need to the best practitioner to help them. Think of it as an eHarmony for mental health and wellness, guided by the power of story.

As a filmmaker myself, Dave and I also believed my show *Sounds of Freedom*, which features the plight of soldiers with PTSD, as well as the documentary stories I continue to produce could provide much-needed therapy for mental health patients in a new, reimagined, interactive format. Instead of the traditional documentary structure that follows a specific narrative, StoryGuide.ai – adapted from CareSpace – would tailor the story to the individual patient based on the insights and understandings coming from artificial intelligence and machine learning. This would serve as a form of digital therapeutics, helping patients to comprehend and process their mental health issues. However, I see this as a later phase of the project.

My ultimate goal for StoryGuide.ai is to provide

opportunities for anyone to seek out guidance in a fun and easy way. I want this service to be kind, to help people destigmatize their own feelings about mental health, and to assist them in understanding that they may have some difficulty dealing with the heaviness of the challenges we face in this new normal. Through telling stories, a person can share exactly what they are struggling with and then be guided to practitioners who specialize in those issues. I know from experience that sharing your story is healing, and through StoryGuide.ai I strive to give people the ability to seek out services to support them as a result of that story.

Recently, some of my own experiences have inspired some resources we can add to this project. My husband and I sold our beloved boat in July of 2020 in exchange for seeking out security. Because our forty-foot RV is too heavy to haul with our truck, we purchased a toy hauler trailer to carry our desert buggy and set ourselves up in an RV park outside of Blue Ridge, Georgia – completely across country from our beloved Pacific Northwest. Why Georgia, you ask? My husband works in the Gulf of Mexico and had been commuting to Louisiana every three weeks. With the pandemic as a new normal, air travel is not our preferred mode of transportation. This move brought him closer to his work and therefore made his commute easier. Wanting a secure home base, we soon put an offer in for a log home in the woods in Northern Georgia. Having a dream and a dream house is my way of being kind to myself. If I have to live in the southern United States – which, as someone native to Washington, feels like a foreign land to me – I should do it in a place that makes me happy. If anything, this pandemic has taught me to be adaptable, to stay attuned to my emotional and mental needs, and to be kind to myself.

One day, about four weeks after we arrived in Blue Ridge,

I was sitting in the RV park clubhouse taking advantage of the high-speed internet when I heard machine gun fire through the woods. I was pretty sure machine guns were illegal, but I noticed that no one at the clubhouse batted an eyelash. Two weeks later, someone at the clubhouse mentioned that there was a business named Tank City across the street where you could drive tanks, crush cars, and fire machine guns. Okay, so that explains what I heard, but it still showed I had arrived in an American culture that celebrated destruction.

At first, I was uncomfortable with these unavoidable signs of being surrounded by a culture I didn't fit into. Then I thought, it's okay to be uncomfortable during this time of uncertainty. That's a very real reaction. It's okay to grieve, to miss Washington, and to not be positive about everything. It's okay to have uncertainty about living in the South and making it my home base. It's okay to sit with this uncertainty and feel nervous. It's more important to be conscious of my fear, and then to live my life from a place of wholehearted love. I was proud of this conclusion and my shift to acknowledging the uncertainty I was feeling instead of ignoring it like I had done in my past. As I documented this in my book and researched it with Rubi, I was also proud of my work with Rubi to assure me that this was truth. I was working to expand the abilities of technology, to train it to pick up on the meaningful connections humans make that may not necessarily be logical, and to dive into the realm of the spiritual. I don't know how possible it is for machine learning to pick up on these connections since they are different for everyone, but at the very least, I hope to train something non-human that can connect with humanity and can provide a variety of educational perspectives. And by doing so, I will help people around the world improve their mental health. It's better to be real and love fully than be considered normal and live in fear.

After coming to this realization, I researched some educational content to potentially include as reference material for StoryGuide.ai that could help others in similar situations. *Welcoming the Unwelcome: Wholehearted Living in a Brokenhearted World* by Buddhist nun Pema Chodron struck me as a worthy resource to include. The book certainly helped me know that pursuing a wholehearted perspective on life despite the unwelcome and the unknown is essential not only for healing, but also for happiness. Another resource was humanitarian and psychotherapist Jennifer van Wyck's book *The Good Thing about Mortar Shells: Choosing Love over Fear.* In it, the author shares how she has gone into the most extreme and hostile situations, including the Ebola outbreak; how she chose to lead, live, and handle these situations with love instead of fear; and how doing so made a drastic difference in her patients' lives.

StorygGuide.ai is still in the early stages. After applying to an emergency relief fund and getting rejected, I was invited to fundraise on WeFunder – a platform targeted to vetted investors – once I raise some seed money. I am hoping this seed money will come from my own collaborative book, which will be comprised of ambassador StoryGuide storytellers who have struggled with mental illness or a spiritual crisis, are grappling with a new normal, or are a provider who offers a revolutionary wellness service and are willing to be the first to try out the platform. I still feel like a movie star in a movie lot trailer, waiting for her next scene. These are all dreams, but they are dreams in motion. I have memorized my part and have the greenlight for production!

I don't wear my pajamas regularly on walks anymore. Oh, you may catch me in them as I take the dogs out for an early morning pee, but otherwise my dressing habits are back to normal. What is not back to normal is the foreign sounds of our new log home. It'll take time to feel settled, but with the house having fewer square feet than my childhood home and being set in the forest with no yard to maintain, I believe I have found a balance between security, focus, creativity, and adventure. And as I look to the future, I'm excited for where my next steps will take me.

A new global story is emerging – one that you are already a part of. These are uncertain and sometimes terrifying times, and you may feel alone and isolated. I encourage you to share your story of hope, survival, trials, and tribulations during these unprecedented times. Storytelling – either in a collaborative book, on StoryGuide.ai, or in one-on-one conversations – is an important part of the healing process, and it can help you connect with others in so many ways. I hope you join me in telling your story, wherever and however you choose, so we can shift our whole word towards healing.

About Holly Chadwick

Holly was raised by her grandparents, who believed in rigorous music studies. Though she didn't become a concert pianist, she has directed short movies, documentaries, and now the Amazon show, *Sounds of Freedom*, which was inspired by her father and his battle with PTSD. At the age of sixteen, Holly was a key member in a successful Internet start-up and went on to working for fine art and newspaper publishing companies in design and advertising, as well as in a darkroom developing crime scene photos. She earned a BA in Film and Digital Media from the University of California, Santa Cruz and has studied fine art and digital media as far away as Italy and The Banff Centre in Alberta, Canada.

Holly resides in Northwest Georgia in a log home with her husband and two golden retrievers. She enjoys kayaking, boating, playing piano, photography and off-roading adventures. She is also working on a memoir featuring her mother, mental illness, and herself called My New Normal. You can follow her projects at the links below.

www.eideticfilm.com
www.soundsoffreedomtheseries.com
www.storyguide.ai
Facebook: facebook.com/soundsoffreedomtheseries/
Facebook: facebook.com/hollyjeanchadwick/
Twitter: @freedom_of
Twitter: @holly_chadwick
Instagram: @hollyjeanchadwick/
Instagram: @soundsoffreedomtheseries/

4

The Beauty in the Simple Things

by Lorna Ketler

"We are encouraged to obsess over our instrument's SHAPE — but our body's shape has no effect on it's ability to accept and offer love for us. Just none. Maybe we continue to obsess because as long we keep wringing our hands about our paintbrush shape, we don't have to get to work painting our lives. Stop fretting. The truth is that all paintbrush shapes work just fine — and anybody who tells you different is trying to sell you something. Don't buy it. Follow your heart and paint!"
Glennon Doyle

The Beauty in the Simple Things

By Lorna Ketler

I was ready for 2020 to be filled with celebration. I was turning fifty-five; my clothing store, Bodacious, was turning twenty years old; and my hubby and I were reaching thirty years of loving each other. We had the hall and the band booked so we could celebrate and dance with our friends and family. Unfortunately, these celebrations would have to wait.

It started with a buzz and some gentle warnings. Cautions were put out into the community, and we all started washing our hands in earnest, joked about not hugging each other, and got a wee bit paranoid about any cough or sneeze.

Then, things got real. It felt like everything shifted overnight. My hubby kept working through it all, so we knew we had to keep our bubble very small. We stopped seeing friends, and for at least three months we only visited my mother-in-law through her patio doors. To minimize my exposure, I stopped going to the grocery store and let George do all our shopping – I'll admit to liking that particular part of our new reality. As much as we love to explore different restaurants throughout the city, all our meals were now taken home. The hardest part for me was that people stopped coming into my boutique clothing store, and I had to lay off my staff. As difficult as this decision was, everyone was very understanding of my situation. We all hoped this was only temporary, but I couldn't make any promises. There was still so much unknown.

I may have spent an afternoon under the covers, wondering what the hell I would do to survive this pandemic if it lasted any length of time. Okay, I actually did do that. And then, like any true entrepreneur, I got out of bed, put on my big girl panties, and got to work.

I'd been wanting to put my business online in a bigger way for years but had never made it a priority. Now it was no longer optional. I spent my days connecting with my customers through newsletters and live posts on social media, keeping them informed about what was happening as much as I could. These posts weren't always about new fashions, but instead were more of a check-in and chat about life and my experience being in the store, and I still keep them up to this day. I do my best to offer that warm smile on the other side of the computer screen, and I always get great feedback when I share what's going on for me.

A more challenging project was moving my sales online – if I couldn't get this working, I'd be in serious trouble. Thankfully, I was already set up to sell online so I didn't have to reinvent the wheel. The program we use to sell in store is called Shopify, and I just had to add details and photos of the products and click some buttons to make everything available to a much wider audience.

I started taking pictures of myself in the outfits and posting them to my online store, and I immediately saw a healthy response. This gave me some reassurance that I could survive this unexpected turn of events. In truth, though, I was not surprised that my customers supported me as it has always been my goal to build relationships with the wonderful women who shop in my store. Having been in business for twenty years now, I'm fortunate to have a strong and supportive group of customers. That being said, it still truly warmed my heart to know that these women had my back. And of course, they already knew I had a great selection of clothing for the coming spring season and loved being able to see them on an actual body so they could picture how the clothes would work for them.

As well as offering shipping, I started a free personal delivery service to my local customers. There were many chats across front porches and gardens as I dropped off lovely pink bags filled with fashion. I felt like it was a new and welcomed way to connect and check in with how everyone was doing. I think we all appreciated each other more in these moments; the lack of connection was hurting us all.

Full disclosure here: I had an incredible amount of support to help me get through this challenging period, something I am aware does not exist for everyone. My business landlord talked to me in the very early days of the shutdown and said he'd do whatever was necessary to make sure I survived this. I applied for and received the government loans offered, including the personal income support from our local government. Phew! I also have friends who check in regularly and a wonderful, supportive life partner. This made me feel like I could do what needed to be done to get through this, and yet it was still hard and super scary.

I feel like I'm sharing this experience with so many other

small retailers. In the early days of the pandemic, I made a point of reaching out to other retailers to offer support and check in. It brought me strength and comfort to know that I was not alone in this. We've all been just putting one foot in front of the other and surviving day by day, trying to make the wisest decisions we can in the face of so many unknowns.

I had to attend to my business quickly and put some plans in place to respond to the immediate situation, but of course there was so much more to think about. I had gotten used to having a team; now I was working solo again, and I was lonely. I was worried about my family and friends – we were able to keep connected through Zoom calls, but that wasn't enough. I also needed to make sure I was taking care of my own mental health; I needed to be creative. So, I reignited my passion for making bead jewelry and started playing around with paints. I signed up for a few online painting and jewelry making classes to get the creative juices flowing. I gave myself the time and permission to sit at my table and play with colour, texture, and design.

My immediate goal was to create and get out of my head, but new ideas started creeping in. I started designing earrings, necklaces, and other gift items that I could sell in-store and online – something I'd done twenty-five years earlier at outdoor farmers markets. I also had my art printed onto a variety of items such as cosmetic bags, shopping bags, and pillowcases. It was so much fun! I started to feel like I was bringing my business inward. I've been curating product for my store for two decades, and I still love doing it, but I now have a desire to curate from within as well – more local, more personal, more of my own creations. This has been another shift that has evolved during these chaotic times, and it stirred up a creative side that I'd kept pushed down for too long.

The online business and home delivery sales were sufficient to pay the rent, which left me with a strange sense of freedom. Instead of feeling more stressed about next steps, I was enjoying the easier days which allowed time for me to explore what I really wanted to do.

With my business more-or-less on a stronger track, the next hugely important consideration was my mom. She was living alone in Vancouver, and while it was only a ferry ride away from Victoria, it might as well have been on the moon once things began shutting down. Even though she had family nearby, the pandemic meant that her contact with the outside world was very limited. This was keeping me up at night. She was able to go out a bit more and have some social interactions once the restrictions started to lift, but this situation had planted the seed that I wanted her closer. I wanted to know that if things shut down again, she'd be in my bubble. Also, my mom and I had started to develop a new and closer relationship over the past several years, and I wanted to nourish that.

After a lot of discussion, the three of us – my hubby, my mom, and I – decided to start looking for a place we could all live together. Thankfully, my husband was incredibly supportive. We had some pretty specific needs as my mom uses a walker and can't deal with stairs, so I put my thoughts/wishes into the universe and trusted that there would be a perfect home for us out there. I even drew a picture of what this home would look like: a pretty ranch-style house with a yard, a garden space, and a garage for storage. Well, I'm in the middle of writing this story on a lakeside holiday, just days before we go to pick up my mom to come and live with us in the three-bedroom house that we found to share together. And funny enough, it looks a lot like my picture!

This is a huge leap of faith and love for each of us, and

I'm thrilled, excited, and nervous. I haven't lived with my mom since I was a teenager, and my hubby and I have never shared our home with anyone. Adjusting to this new living situation will be a significant process. Setting new boundaries, practicing patience, and dedicating time for myself will be important now more than ever. There will be challenges, but we're going to meet them together, and I'm feeling blessed to have this time to spend with my mom.

Over the past six months, I've learned that life is really about the moments, and I'm putting my focus on marking them, appreciating them, and remembering that the hard times pass. Knowing that I'm near enough to help my mom, and that she won't be alone during any potential pandemic restrictions, does so much to ease my mind.

Life is starting to make its way back to some semblance of normal. I've been able to bring my staff back a couple of days per week, but it's still primarily just me in the store. Again, there's a lovely ease in the simplicity of it all. I feel like I was pulled back to the roots of why I do what I do: offering a beautiful space for women to find their own style while having time for family and other artistic pursuits, including my own line of Bodacious clothing.

The growth of my business is not my priority right now, but strength is. Streamlining is. Flexibility is. Beauty is. I'm so proud of what my team and I have achieved, especially in these challenging times. We provide an environment of safety, celebration, and fun for women to find their own creative style with beautiful clothing options from around the world, and I will continue to do this with passion and dedication.

As we navigate our way around this new reality, the words that keep resonating for me are "blessed" and "blend." So many parts of my life are blending together in an organic way. Trusting in next steps, leading with love, being open to creativity, and building this new version of our lives together helps me know that we're on the right path. Also, I'm so blessed to have this time with my mom while also reconnecting to my core passion and my why's. I'm loving the slowdown to a more natural rhythm. I'm finding the beauty in the simple things and celebrating the moments – a hug from mom, morning swims in our local lake, the sunrise, dancing in the kitchen, colourful beads and paints.

In the early days of the pandemic, it was hard to see anything positive. As we all scrambled to keep up with the daily changes and updates, my priority was just keeping my family and myself safe. But soon, I came to realize that within this, there was a much bigger opportunity being shown to me. I took the time to pay closer attention to how I want to be living my life and who I want to spend it with, and now my life has improved in so many ways. By embracing this opportunity for change, I have reignited long-forgotten passions and brought my family closer together. When if felt like so much could be taken away in a moment, I'm grateful that I was reminded of what really matters.

About Lorna Ketler

Lorna Ketler is the owner and lead body-love enthusiast at Bodacious Lifestyles Inc, a women's clothing store that offers a fun, safe, welcoming environment where all bodies are beautiful and worthy of being celebrated. Her store is located in Victoria, BC, but can also be found online and at various pop-up shops throughout the lower mainland. Through her store, and through her online presence, she passionately encourages women to fully recognize and appreciate their beauty, their bodies, and their curves.

Lorna delights in seeing the world from a fresh perspective. As she approached fifty, she decided that she would create an "epic" experience each month over the course of a year, starting with walking one hundred kilometres of the Camino de Santiago on her fiftieth birthday. She then filled her months with big and small experiences including jewelry making classes, painting workshops, travel, and most importantly, spending precious time with dear friends.

Celebrating twenty years in business this year, Lorna plans to enjoy that accomplishment by exploring new adventures and opportunities, including making art and having a big, bodacious dance party! After five years of living on her boat, Lorna now enjoys living in beautiful Victoria, BC, with her husband and best friend George.

www.bodacious.ca

5

Trust in the Process of Life

by Karen Angelucci

*"Your body is your birthright,
love and care for your body!
Life is precious,
embrace living fulfilled daily."*
Karen Angelucci

Trust in the Process of Life

By Karen Angelucci

Making sense of my life experiences drives my curious nature, feeds my awe in the mysteries of my body, and rekindles the reverence I have for life. Emotional chaos, confusion about what to eat, nutritional deficiencies, and the physical pains I've experienced have led me to question my circumstances, be curious about my options, and make choices towards health recovery. And what I started noticing years ago was that the times I experienced inner turmoil were also the times when the magic happened in my life – so long as I was willing to do the self-discovery needed to navigate the volatility, uncertainty, complexity, and anxiety that overwhelmed me.

As I wrote this chapter, I reflected on the sixty-five years I have lived and the mind/body shifts I've made. One of the biggest shifts came in my early thirties, when I was a single mom of a five-year-old. I was running on overdrive, experiencing adrenal exhaustion, riding an emotional roller coaster, and feeling at a complete loss as to who I was, how to be a parent, and what direction I was supposed to take. Even though I felt like I was a victim of my circumstances, subconsciously I knew I needed to change. I took a leap of faith and signed up for a twenty-eight-day residential self-development program – and believe me, taking that step was a life-altering leap of faith. I knew nothing of what was to come as I made sure my daughter was in good care, packed my bag, and headed off to live on an island with people I had never met. I shared a room with other participants, we ate our meals together, and we attended ongoing self-discovery sessions. This extended time away from my day-to-day routines started me on a foundational path of trusting in the process of life and looking to nature as my resource.

I didn't know how much I needed this shift in mindset until years later, when I looked back at how the direction of my life evolved after I removed myself from the paradigm I was living in and created space for growth and self-care. Since then, I have continued to develop the physical, emotional, and nutritional skillsets I need for my own wellbeing and have turned them into a career as a body-centred practitioner, trusted by clients for the past twenty-five years to help initiate their self-discovery and health recovery processes.

This same uncertainty and volatility is exactly what I witnessed as the components of the historic 2020 pandemic unfolded, forcing all our social structures to shift. During this time, my lifestyle choices were more restricted than I was accustomed to. It's one thing to make life changes because of personal needs, as I had done in the past. But in this global state of fear and confusion, I got caught up in thinking about what I was supposed to do, how I could be safe, and how I was going to transition my work from in-person to online. All the escalated media coverage and medical catastrophizing heightened the perceived threats of what was to come, which overrode the logic I needed to assess my actual situation.

All of this was made worse by being told to social distance. Going for walks in my neighbourhood or lining up to shop at the local vegetable market was like going through a maze of zombies; people would not talk or make eye contact for fear they would catch something. This made no sense to me – staying six feet apart didn't mean we had to ignore each other entirely – and I worried that this fear of one another was going to cause more unwarranted emotional distress. I made a point of saying hello to people and making eye contact to help combat this. Thankfully, after many months, the media adopted a new message of maintaining physical distance while remaining socially and emotionally connected. Be calm, kind, and safe has become the slogan on many signs.

Within a week of shutting down my in-person business, I was frantically searching the Internet on how to make videos so I could sustain an income. A techie I am not. The endless hours I spent watching do-it-yourself videos and webinars created a frenzied tension in me. Taking a break to surf Facebook was a delightful distraction. I got to see people acting out their emotional overload through humorous posts, pictures of people making bread, and many other ways friends and family were spending their time in an effort to override the stressors from the forced changes they had to navigate. I loved the motivational posts that kept the thread of connectedness for me and gave me perspective, especially one quote that brought me back to my reality: "Even though we are all in the same ocean, we are not in the same boat!" In essence, for some people this storm was going to have devastating, life-altering consequences while others could simply put their sail up and ride the waves to calmer waters.

As I checked in with my own weather conditions and really examined the boat-in-the-ocean analogy, I remembered that I am fully equipped to deal with the physical tension and anxiety I was conjuring with my "what if" scenarios. The self-discovery and growth that I have gained from dealing with past personal crises have taught me to be self-sufficient, resilient, creative, and capable of releasing my own physical and emotional tension.

To help move myself forward, I sat with and examined what I was feeling – especially my frustrations around closing my private practice. I have a studio where I provide Pilates active rehabilitation and fitness programs combined with manual and integrative health techniques. I quickly realized my frustration was not about having to shut down – as a one-person, home-based studio, my loss of income was nothing compared to those who had commercial overhead and staff. It was because I knew that if I was feeling tense and stressed, others were as well. I am driven to help individuals move, feel, and live better in their body, both now and into the future, and I knew that what I needed and wanted to do was to continue sharing my skills. I am determined to expand my sphere of influence and pursue my vision of helping people create their health action plan and making body health simple. This is where I am focusing my inspiration, energy, and time.

Unfortunately, the hands-on approach that I use in my studio didn't fit into this new online world, and it quickly became apparent that creating videos or webinars – something I had seen many other people achieve in a short period of time – wasn't my forte. And that's okay. I'm a work in progress. There will be challenges in switching my in-person business to an online format, and I will need help in the areas I can't figure out for myself. In the meantime, I continue to do work on myself so that I can grow during these tumultuous times.

Learning about my body has always been an amazing resource for deepening my understanding of life and enhancing my career. The studio closure afforded me time to connect with my interests, and I decided to use this time to take an online anatomy dissection course. Seeing the body from the inside out can be a very emotional experience, and fortunately the anatomist teaching the course had the ability to share his reverence of the body with compassion and awe. And during this lesson, there was one thing he shared that really stood out to me as being relevant to this time. As he held the heart in his hands, still attached in the chest cavity, he talked about the heart's presence circulating through the entirety of our body as the blood nourishes all our cells – thank you, heart, for the endless work you do without me thinking about it! He also explained that each breath we take oxygenates the blood our heart delivers throughout our body, and that the heart is inherently designed in a way that it feeds itself the oxygenated blood first. Hearing this gave me pause, and I immediately saw the lesson I was meant to take from it: I must love and care for myself first, just like my physical heart does, before I can love and care for others. I took this awesome message as permission to continue to embrace self-care as I explore the birthright of my body and my relationship with nature.

Standing up, claiming my space, and being myself in business are the next steps in my adventure. As I work on this, I am reminded of a lesson I learned in the past. Again, I was at a body workshop and the instructor emphatically instilled in me that gravity is proof that we belong on this Earth. This message came to me at a time when I felt like I did not belong, and it led me to accept that no other person occupies my place – that it is mine to claim. I belong here, and I am meant to share the lessons I've learned.

I've felt constraints around moving forward with my goals because I didn't know the steps needed to accomplish what I want or felt that asking for help was cost-prohibitive. The challenges of asking for and receiving help in business are my upcoming lessons. But one step I know I can take is to share some of my lessons with you, here, in this chapter.

Being in survival mode for extended periods of time has numerous negative impacts on our body's health, which affects our relationships and our ability to think clearly. Seeing this virus as something that we can only be protected from by outside powers, such as a vaccine, limits our personal choices. I have witnessed the debilitating consequences for people who felt they had no control over their body or health, and in my experience, we have two options in this scenario: to find ways to empower ourselves, or to become apathetic. I am grateful for the worldwide efforts of so many to uncover the best ways to aid our body in recovering from this virus or prevent it from spreading, but for me, there is also a personal responsibility to make choices that will support our immune function and physical resiliency.

I have been biologically blessed with a body that is my motorhome, all its moving parts working together to take me where I want to go and help me experience life. And an important part of being able to go on this journey of discovery is to take care of the vessel that is moving me through it. Being an active participant in making decisions that support, serve, and enrich my life has emboldened me. The difficulty is I don't always know what I need, and just like with my business, I'll quite likely need help discerning what actions steps to take.

However, the awesome fact remains I have choices in the three essential areas that control my wellbeing: physical, emotional, and nutritional.

Our body heals from the inside out. For example, when you cut yourself, your body has the innate ability to stop the bleeding, close the cut, and rebuild the tissue. Of course, if any of our body's natural healing processes are compromised or the injury is extreme, then we will need interventions to assist these processes. But it is not the bandage or the antibacterial cream creating the healing – they are simply tools to support your body as it heals itself.

Similarly, each of us has individual physical, emotional, and nutritional (PEN) needs to support our body in staying as healthy as possible. How we attend to those needs will require attention to our self-care, help-care and healthcare.

Healthcare involves knowing the specifics about your personal PEN health. For example, I recently discovered I am predisposed to diabetes; this information helps me make dietary choices that will prevent me from developing this condition. Another example is that I found out through genetic testing that I need to take a Vitamin B complex daily for my cells to produce energy effectively – without it, I feel drained and lethargic. Knowing what your health needs are is vital to creating and taking action steps.

Self-care is the skills you have or need that allow you to look after your body. For instance, when I was in my twenties, I fell six feet and landed on my tailbone. I didn't know who to go to or what to do at the time, so to this day, my tailbone is vulnerable and I can easily develop tension in my lower back. Through my work, I see many people suffering from past injuries or accidents, and generally they don't attend to their alignment or explore movement practices. The ensuing body stiffness affects the circulation of blood, lymph, and energy, creating increased soreness or rigidity which then contributes to additional health consequences. To prevent this, I stretch and do exercises on a regular basis and visit an osteopath as needed to help me get into alignment and move better.

Finally, help-care is knowing who to go to when you don't know what's going on with your health or what to do for self-care. There are many health practitioners available to you, each with their own paradigm of treatment, so I suggest you find one that can support your specific PEN needs. Because of my history of injuries, genetic predispositions, and nutritional health needs, an integrative approach best helps me attend to my personal health. The core team of practices I turn to are osteopaths, naturopaths, medical doctors, or counsellors depending on the circumstance. Your choices would be different because you have your own unique needs. However, always remember that practitioners don't fix you! Just like a bandage protects a wound to support its healing, practitioners create the environment or opportunity that engages your body to do its own healing.

While the pandemic has created uncertainty, fear, distress, and upheaval for many, it has also been an opportunity for us to reflect and draw on our resilience, strengths, and internal compass to find a new vision and begin co-creating our health, relationships, and businesses. For me, a door opened to share my vision, insights, and skills. Writing a chapter in this book has been one step toward being visible. I am also taking a leap of faith and answering the call to action to help others with their health and wellbeing by offering online workshops and public speaking.

We are inextricably linked with the cycles of nature – we grow, develop, mature, and die. How we experience this will depend on the choices we make. I am grateful that I can make choices that allow me to embrace living a fulfilling life, and I feel blessed that I have spent the time, energy, and money needed to attend to my wellbeing.

Your body is your birthright, and as you understand and care for your body's physical, emotional, and nutritional health, you become a co-creator and contributing force for vibrant living in your body, your family, your community, and around the world. Trust in the process of life, and you may experience a mind/body shift that you never thought possible.

About Karen Angelucci

Curiosity about the human body drives Karen's passion. As a Health Creation Coach trusted by clients for over twenty-five years, she helps you make body health simple. By creating your health action plan with self-care skills, knowing who to go to for help-care, and discerning what your healthcare needs are, individuals are empowered to care for their body and improve their quality of life at all ages.

Karen has learned that it's possible to open the door to healing from the inside out. She emboldens you with skills to learn about your body, educates you to make choices to care for yourself, and inspires you to take action. Pilates-certified in 1995 and currently completing her osteopathic studies, she combines integrative health techniques in her private practice in South Surrey.

As an international speaker, Karen engages her audience with experiences that guide them to new awareness of their body. Her vision is to help you break through the fears you may have about your body, especially around aging, and to invest in your "birthright" physically, emotionally, and nutritionally.

www.birthrightinvestment.com
Facebook: Birthright Investment
LinkedIn: Karen Angelucci
Email: hello@birthrightinvestment.com

6

Finding the Positive

by Shelly Lynn Hughes

*"You can't always control what goes on outside.
But you can always control what goes on inside."*
Wayne Dyer

Finding the Positive

By Shelly Lynn Hughes

As an entrepreneur, pivoting is an inevitable part of the long journey to success. This year, we were all simultaneously forced to pivot as the world came up against an invisible foe in the form of this formidable virus. Networking, marketing, events, and business as we knew them came to a very scary halt, and then what felt like a collective moment passed where we all held our breath and paused to reassess and re-strategize how we live our lives and run our businesses.

Personally, my team and I had a major nation-wide project in the works with only the final details to solidify before launching into a new stratosphere with an exciting trajectory. We were gearing up to launch a speaker series and photoshoot publicity opportunity. The idea was to showcase successful women in business and give them a platform to celebrate their successes. We had crews and an initial group of speakers lined up in three provinces. Everyone was enthusiastic about the plan, and we were in the process of finalizing the team. That all came to a screeching halt in March, and I was left wondering – how long will this last? When can we get back to it? What now? I believe that big ideas require strategic but quick moves, so this pause alone was a big shift for me. But in that same breath-holding moment, I found myself able to reflect and reprioritize. That's when everything changed.

My businesses fuel me, but I also have two amazing kids who give me life. I was just coming back from a trip to New York City with my eldest daughter when things started to really get serious. Before I left, there were rumblings of what was to come but no concrete warnings other than a few concerned friends who told me not to go on my trip. However, my eldest daughter had a dream of seeing Beetlejuice on Broadway, and this was supposed to be the trip of a lifetime for the two of us. Maybe I was naïve, maybe I was choosing to be optimistic, but I made the decision to take the trip with her and I couldn't be happier about it. Two days after we got back to Vancouver, BC, the pandemic really started for us and everything locked down. A month later, the entirety of NYC shut down and Broadway stopped all their shows. In hindsight, it was potentially a risky decision to go on that trip, but if we hadn't, we may never have had the opportunity to fulfill one of my daughter's dreams. So, I choose to view it as extremely fortunate timing that we were able to share that experience and make it back safely.

By June, many people were starting to settle into the idea that this pandemic was here for the long haul and we weren't going to see our lives go back to "normal" any time soon. It was a time of mass reflection. We were all forced to prioritize not only the people we chose for our "bubble," but also our spending habits, daily routines, and family activities all at once. The whole country was buzzing with what-ifs, and there was a juxtaposition between the calm and stillness of the lockdown and the subtle panic of the uncertainty we were facing. It was a very long make-or-break moment in so many ways, and with me being who I am, I took this as an opportunity to completely overhaul my business and home and launch myself towards the future I wanted for myself using the tools I could control.

I started by going through my entire home and doing a massive purge, which leaned into the reset feeling I was craving and cleared my headspace for a deep dive into my businesses – my other babies. I analyzed what was working and what was not and had to decide what I needed to do to adapt. Through this process, I was able to dive into this incredibly positive space and found myself re-energized. I could handle this.

After a deep cleanse and rallying of resources, I find it best to zoom out and take a look at the big picture. This is what I can't do, this is what I can. This is what I can't control, this is what I can – and it doesn't serve me to panic over the things I can't. This affirmation allowed me to focus, concentrate, and plan my revamp. I was gearing up for change, and it was going to be good.

During this time of purging and resetting, I was also spending time with my kids on a new schedule, which was a completely new experience for all of us. My eldest daughter has severe allergies and a weakened immune system, so she's higher risk and takes this pandemic quite seriously. She was already homeschooled so her bubble was relatively tightknit, which made the transition to this year's situation a lot smoother. She is diligent about wearing a mask and careful about keeping to her bubble. We definitely had some anxiety about the situation, but she is championing through. My other daughter is four, so she's young enough that this has all just become normal for her. She is used to wearing a mask now and treats it like it's just what you do when you go into a store. She has her playdates over video chat, and it's fun and normal. Both of my kids have handled being home more and seeing their friends less or through virtual means so well, and they have stayed calm throughout everything. I worked hard to set a good example for how to react to a crisis, and I believe I succeeded. We talked about what was happening, made our adjustments, and have continued living our lives with those adjustments in the best way we can.

As summer came to a close and the back-to-school thoughts began, people were looking at the numbers being shared in the news and getting nervous. There was much debate around whether kids should physically go to school or stay home and do virtual learning. This decision is personal and complex, but I knew that it would do my youngest more harm than good to keep her out of school. Not only does it better serve her mental and social health, but as a single mom I have to make money to support my kids, which means that having the time and space to run my businesses is also a priority. Children don't just need a new, autonomous routine; they need socialization, structure, and ideally a separated space for learning. I knew it would be a challenge for me to provide that, so it was important that I got my daughter back into school when the time came, recognizing that the precautions in place were an equal priority.

My businesses were also preparing to change. When a little more of our area opened up, my revamp plans really started to be implemented. We purged, we pivoted, we strategized, and now it was time to act. For one of the businesses I co-own, Project Her, we decided to transition our live speaker series to an online format, found a digital partner, and reconfigured the team for a digital structure. Our first virtual event went really well, and now we are ready to announce a monthly speaker series with an online membership. The magazine was ready for a refresh, and our newly designed digital site is launching soon. I also have a book coming out in 2021 celebrating businesswomen across the country called Pursuit: 365 that will be distributed nationally, and we're beyond excited to be honouring these amazing women.

All things considered, I've come out of quarantine in a better position than I've possibly ever been. As a single mom and an owner of multiple businesses, life was usually too hectic for me to sit down and reflect enough to develop these amazing realizations and project goals and really build up my team. Now all my companies are structured, smooth, and building steadily to be bigger and stronger. This forced pause has its silver linings, and it's amazing what we've been able to accomplish with some time and distance from our previous daily routines.

Reflecting on 2020 thus far, it's been a steady process of pause, collect, pivot, purge, and build. There has been a lot of fear about government control and conspiracy theories running around the internet; there is often something very real behind that fear, and I want to be cognizant of those things. But I also appreciate that we all have been able to step back and look at our lives on a deeper level, and that everyone is appreciating the small things a bit more. There's something really human and beautiful about that.

In the early days of the pandemic, my eagerness to take on new projects and expand rapidly created a life of go-go-go that was probably unsustainable but also provided so many opportunities for me – and besides, I didn't know how else to be! Now, a few months into this "new-and-shifting normal,"

I've come out of it with resilience and vigour. I take everything one day at a time, and I try to find the positive in everything. I can't control the pandemic, but I can control what goes on in my own home and what I do with my time and mental space. I can control how I deal with what is happening. I can encourage the people around me to stay calm and steady and use the opportunities that are presented to them to pivot and change their own lives for the better. That's how I move forward – focusing in on the things I can control.

I have to say that even with everything that is going on, right now I feel amazing. I'm busy doing my own thing and trying to help the people around me. I am consumed with finding the light in everything around me – maybe that's a negative sometimes, but I don't dwell on negative things. Seeing my kids be so strong and so responsible through a very serious global situation is incredibly gratifying. Knowing that they are keeping calm and doing their part to keep themselves and everyone around them safe is a proud mom moment. And I know that at least part of that has come from the example I have set for them. The time to reflect gave me the space to acknowledge the power I have over my life and my kids' futures, and the work I've done on my businesses over the last six months has been incredibly validating of those endeavours.

Reigniting my purpose, sustaining my passion for my businesses and family, and coming into my power in my own life in this extraordinary time is a day-by-day process. I'm thinking and using my head. I'm not going to be reckless, but I'm not panicking and getting stuck into those moments. With my eldest daughter's allergies, I've had to deal with life-threatening situations her whole life. In the beginning I would panic, but that became more dangerous than not panicking. In order to find a positive outcome, I needed to learn to move forward calmly and positively. This same lesson applies to the situation we find ourselves in today. If we're not calm while we're dealing with massive things in our lives, then how can we make the proper decisions moving forward? Instead of panicking, we should sit down and ask ourselves what we can do today to make our futures better.

So, my last words to anyone looking for that stroke of inspiration or motivation to ignite their own path to a stronger, happier, more successful flip side of a global pandemic: take it one day at a time, reflect, reorganize, and act – and definitely don't panic.

About Shelly Lynn Hughes

Shelly Lynn Hughes is the founder of Fresh Magazine and a partner with Skin Spin Cosmetics, Project Her Inc, and YOYOMAMA.CA. In addition to her work as a publisher and business owner, she has developed an exclusive skincare label for a major pharmacy and consulted for various magazines and health and beauty brands. Shelly was the recipient of the prestigious WOW Woman Of Worth "Mom Entrepreneur of the Year" Award in 2013. She loves to get her hands on an idea, make it a reality, and share it with the world – all while radiating the good vibes of a best girlfriend.

www.freshmag.ca
www.skinspin.com
www.yoyomama.ca
www.projecther.com
Twitter: @iamshellylynn
Instagram: @shellylynn.hughes

7

Put the Mirror Down and Let Yourself Out

by Treva Gambs

*"Women leaders are a valuable asset in any industry ...
[They] lead with a different compassion. And that
provides a profound strength of leadership that is
actually critical to a workforce environment."*
Alana Hughson

Put the Mirror Down and Let Yourself Out

By Treva Gambs

One beautiful August day, I got ready to head into my restaurant as I have for the past decade. I had my morning tea, petted my dogs, and gave them their treat before jumping in the car. The birds were singing, cars were driving past, and people were out walking their pets. I pulled up to the back door and made a plan in my head for what my day would look like. Once I was ready to go, I reached for my briefcase and purse – oh yeah, and my mask. Everything feels so familiar and yet so different.

In March 2020, the world as I have known it for the past fifty-nine years changed overnight. Now we have made it through the shutdowns and the strict social distancing, but life still looks a lot different than it did before. We are all trying to protect ourselves and our loved ones from this virus, yet figuring out exactly what we should be doing can be a challenge. We've been told to wear a mask when visiting indoor public spaces, although there is some controversy over this. Is it safer? Will wearing them cause other problems? Who do we listen to? Personally, I have chosen to do what is mandated, which can change daily, and then trust my instincts. And as we are still, I believe, at the beginning of this storm, there are many more changes to come.

There are days when I long for the way life used to be. I miss seeing people smile – I can still see twinkles of happiness or pangs of sadness in their eyes, but I miss seeing their mouths. I used to hug all my regulars at the restaurants, and now we "air hug." It still says "I love you," but the lack of touch feels impersonal. It has been six months – some say it will be six more, and others say several years. As a businesswoman with two restaurants, I hope for the former but prepare for the latter.

Facing all of the unknowns ahead of us is daunting, and like everyone else, I am scared of what may come. Will I lose my business? Will my family be okay? Will life ever be normal again? If we enter some kind of "new normal," what will that look like? I hope that I will have a happy ending, but it is still too soon to tell. What I can say is that I am enduring, and that I am finding all the silver linings I can. I love learning new things and growing into a better person, and I can certainly say I have grown as a result of living through this pandemic. And one big lesson that has come from this experience is to stop worrying about what I see in the mirror and let my true self shine.

When the pandemic first arrived, our entire lives seemed to move online. I definitely was not ready for that! I chose the restaurant industry because I love personal contact and entertainment. I have been on Facebook for years, but I mostly used it to connect with family and friends or to share food photos and specials for my restaurants. Suddenly, all my face-to-face interactions were happening through Zoom, and it turns out the camera shows everything. My wrinkles look more pronounced than ever, and in my resting face, my jowls look like they belong to a beagle – thankfully they're not as noticeable when I smile, and I am almost always smiling. Unfortunately, smiles do nothing to hide my puffy eyes and double chin. Usually my grey hair is easily fixed, but not so much when all the hairdressers are shut down. It was a harsh reality to face, and I remember thinking, *Really? This is what I need to do?* And the answer was yes. If I wanted to keep my name and business out there, I had to bite the bullet, move out of my comfort zone, and get out of my own way. So I did, and in the process I learned that falling in love with yourself will allow others to fall in love with you, too.

When the shutdowns began, I started doing cooking videos on Facebook live to connect with family and friends. My first video was filmed by a girlfriend who does my payroll and still comes to my office, though we practice social distancing as much as possible. Neither of us really knew how to use the video feature on our phones or how to stream it on Facebook, so I had to google it. Then, right before we were supposed to go live, she had to take a pee break. We finally got going, but we didn't know how to turn the camera so that she could see me. So, she just winged it and followed me as best she could. As soon as I started, though, the whole thing felt so natural. I have taught many people to cook over the years, including my kids, neighbours, and anyone else who wanted to learn – now I was just doing it for a larger audience. Once we finished, we posted the recording for those who could not join us live. We watched it together and I loved it – I didn't miss a beat or an ingredient.

It wasn't until later, when I watched by myself, that I saw my double chin and my butt. What a chunk! I felt self-conscious, but I was having too much fun to care.

My second video was filmed by my husband, but it was not his favourite thing to do – to the point that both he and my son bought me tripods. So, I filmed the third video myself, which was even funnier. I had done some research on videos and learned that filming horizontally shows better on computer screens. What I did not know was that for Facebook live, the video needs to be vertical. So, my whole third video was filmed and streamed sideways. The comments were hilarious. Everyone was posting for me to turn my camera, and then my very talented hairdresser chimed in and informed them that I wasn't going to see their messages – that I didn't have my glasses on and was blind as a bat without them. The one friend said "I got this" and shared that she had her laptop set up sideways. It may not have been a perfect video, but at least we all got a laugh out of it!

There were other lessons that came along as I continued to make these videos. At the beginning of this process, I didn't have to go shopping as the restaurants had lots of products that needed to be used up. I finally went to the grocery store about a month in, and I was shocked to see that the shelves were empty. In all my years, I had never seen anything like it, and I will never forget that feeling or take having food available for granted. I realized that not everyone could get all the ingredients I was using, so I began showing my audience how to make the dishes with whatever they could find.

My videos began to take off as my followers shared them with their family and friends. My competitors saw what I was doing and followed suit, and many of them mentioned that I was a tough act to follow. My natural positivity kept showing through, even during these difficult times. I still have people tell me how much I helped them in the beginning. They loved my smile, that I was willing to share trade secrets, and that I was having fun with them. Through this experience, I learned to relax and let my true self show – not just in person, but on video as well. I made it past the mirror and let my passion for food, wine, and entertaining shine. Besides, my message was not about a beauty product; it was about breaking bread, sharing meals, and feeding your family. I am now working with a social media company to create an Instagram and YouTube presence. I never would have guessed that I could do this, or that anyone would watch, and yet I have strangers on the street come up to me and tell me how much they like my cooking shows.

I now get very excited when I film. Yes, I try to pick out a cute outfit and do my hair and makeup, but I still look like me – no film crew or makeup artist. That's what my following wants. They don't care what color my hair is or how many chins I have. They see me – the fun, happy cook who wants to share her love for food. By being myself, I have inspired others to not give up, have fun, cook, and enjoy life.

Putting the mirror down sounds easy enough, but it's harder than you would think. I still look at my reflection and see all the things that could be improved. I still try to stay fit, and I continue to colour my hair. I want to feel pretty, although what that means changes depending on how I feel. I want to dress up for date night with my husband and feel sexy. I want to look sharp for business appearances or speaking engagements. But most of all, I want my personality to shine and my passion to overshadow my physical appearance. My focus has changed, and I have learned to love myself even if I need to lose some weight or colour my hair. To help combat these influences, I now start my day on a positive note by saying to myself, "Good morning beautiful, what are we going to do today?"

We all can be our own worst critic, but I am not defined by my appearance – and unless you're a beauty consultant, neither are you. So step away from that mirror and let your tribe see you, both the you in your heart and the beauty you resonate. Your family and tribe can help you build the confidence you may need to tell your story, share your passion, and build your business.

My life has not been perfect – I'm a woman with good days and bad days, and I've had both failures and successes. I've experienced marriage, children, divorce, and the loss of a parent, and through all this I have grown to like – no, love – the woman inside. That's not to say I don't have more work to do. I have learned not to judge people, and while I will still catch myself making comments in my head about how someone looks, I now make an effort to correct myself. I have learned that it is much easier to solve a problem from a positive perspective than from a negative one, but there are still times when I have to work at preventing the uncertainty around me from bringing me down. I still work on putting the mirror down and telling myself I'm beautiful, and while most days it's a piece of cake, there are days when I have to draw on family or friends to remind me that I am good enough just the way I am. As I have made these changes, my inner self has become stronger, my passion has grown, and my business has been climbing.

As I look forward, it is hard to predict what the future will bring. My industry may be changing forever. Some of my managers have had to step down to homeschool their children. Staffing is tough as many are scared to come back to work. People do not have schedules, so we do not know when we will be busy. We have a much higher demand for to-go meals.

In-person dining is mostly done outside, which has worked for these warmer months, but I have no idea what the fall and winter will look like. Whatever it may be, I am excited to bring you new ideas. I will keep looking for the silver linings in these stormy clouds, and I will have fun no matter what the virus does. I will continue to give you knowledge on how to feed your family and keep your life as normal as you can during these challenging times. I will encourage you to taste wine, make memories, and savour the moment. I will be your friend and part of your household. I will count the days until I can hug you with all the love and passion I have.

As I finish this chapter, my life has taken another turn and the lovely state that I live in has caught on fire. Oregon has been engulfed in flames and entire communities have disappeared. I have had large losses during this time, but not as much as those that lost everything. The heart-wrenching videos and stories from family and friends take my breath away. During these last two weeks, I have learned that I can still be a gleam of light and positivity for those in need. I have been knocked down and heartbroken, but not defeated!

This pandemic has ruined lives, businesses, and careers, but it has also taught us that nothing is certain, and that the world is an amazing place. As this virus continues to wreak havoc on the world, as well as the fires that have spread across much of the west coast, we can either wallow in negativity or take a step forward and embrace the new normal. And if we are caught up in appearances, in judgements of ourselves and others, in trying to be someone or something that we are not, we will miss out on so many great opportunities to share our passions and talents with the world. So put down that mirror, let go of perfection, and let everyone see the beauty that lives within you.

About Treva Gambs

Treva Gambs is a restaurant owner, business advocate, and inspirational speaker. She is a thirty-five-year veteran of the hospitality industry, is involved in her local chambers, and is a board member of the Oregon Restaurant Association. She is also a court-appointed special advocate for foster children.

Treva is very passionate about her industry and is politically involved. Her speaking engagements are about opening doors and supporting women in your community. Treva is not only involved in Woman Of Worth but also in several other women's groups, including KNOW (Keizer Network Of Women) and Amazing U.

When Treva is not at the restaurant, you will find her at the lake in the summer – where she loves to ski, surf, and kayak – or up on the ski hill in the winter. She has three wonderful children and two grandchildren so far.

Email: treva@gamberettis.com
Facebook: gamberettis or trevagambs
Instagram: trevajogambs

8

Flying Solo

by Helen (Chome) Horwat

"Through the highs and lows and twisted turns of life, persistence and planning is the route of success."
Chome Horwat

Flying Solo

By Helen (Chome) Horwat

The choices you make throughout your life can make you or break you. However, there are so many decisions to be made at any given moment, and it is sometimes difficult to know the right one from the wrong one. As we move through life and learn from our choices, we can only hope to improve our destiny.

Life can be so glorious, rewarding, and exciting; it can also be extremely difficult, sad, and unforgiving. It is important to do the best you can to prepare yourself for the unexpected. Unfortunately, preparation for life is not taught in schools per se, just like it's not taught how to change a tire, clean your house, open a bank account, or look ahead and be ready for anything unseen. In an ideal world, these insights should come from your parents, but that's not always the case. Sometimes they're learned the hard way; sometimes they are never learned at all.

I've worked for American Airlines for thirty-four years now, and this job has been the best education of my life. It has taught me well in so many different aspects of life, and I am humbled and appreciative of it. I have learned the importance of structure, schedules, on-time performance, camaraderie amongst co-workers, self-respect, patience, and concern for every individual who boards our flights. I have learned to turn the other cheek when faced with rudeness, name-calling, and impatient requests. I have also seen kindness and respect. There are passengers in need of a conversation to help ease their fear, anxiety, or loneliness. There are disabled passengers looking for direction and help. It is always my pleasure to make a person's flying experience the best that it can be.

This job is like no other. We can choose to work forty hours a month or one hundred and fifty – these are hours in the air, not on the ground. We can bid for our schedule to include various cities all over the world, and if we want to visit a specific place but aren't booked to go there, we can swap trips with one another. For example, if I have a trip that has an overnight stop in Rome and I want a Paris trip instead, I just have to find someone who will trade with me. The company provides us with our own hotel room, van service to and from the airport, meals in-flight, and a per diem from the time we leave the gate at the originating airport until the time we return, whether it be a one, two, three, or four-day trip.

I have seen the world, and that in itself is a treasure. People who have not experienced this job cannot imagine the satisfaction to be found in seeing human beings from all over the world in their own habitats and witnessing their traditions and religious beliefs. To see the landscapes and beauty in all these different countries is to know that there is a heaven here on Earth. And although there are language barriers preventing you from verbally communicating with the natives, you know by looking into their eyes that most of them want to help. With their smiles, you feel the warmth of humankind.

I am sixty-six years old, and my plan was to retire at the age of seventy. This is not uncommon – a few of our flight attendants have even worked into their eighties. At our airline we are allowed to collect our pension at the age of sixty-five, collect social security when you become qualified, and also work full time. We call this triple dipping. Many of our flight attendants look forward to doing this for various reasons, and if you have maintained a healthy lifestyle and still enjoy the job, there is no reason not to take advantage of this. Personally, I thought this would be a great way to save some extra money so that I could have a more fun and frivolous lifestyle when I retired.

While I was looking forward to the benefits of this extra income, it was simply going to be a bonus. Since I was hired by the federal government as a clerk-typist at the age of seventeen, I have always planned for the future by saving money and paying cash for everything – thanks, Mom, for that valuable lesson. In the long run, this discipline has paid off. I have had a great life. I have remained single by choice, but I have had wonderful boyfriends. I am totally financially secure with some excellent investments, and have almost always been debt-free. If I had to do it over again, I probably would repeat it the same way. And now, I was setting myself up to enjoy my retirement as much as possible.

In March of 2020, I was ready and eager to start triple dipping. I was already receiving my pension, and I would start collecting my social security at the end of April. And then everything changed.

The World Health Organization was informed of a novel coronavirus on December 31, 2019. On January 30, 2020, the WHO declared this outbreak to be a global health emergency. On March 11, it became a global pandemic. At the time of writing (and it will be higher after publication), this virus – which began in Wuhan, China – had sickened more than twenty-seven million people, and almost 900,000 have died.

The United States' handling of this situation has been questionable, but by the middle of March things started to be taken seriously. On March 12, Ohio was the first in the nation to close schools statewide, and on March 16, President Trump acknowledged the aggressive CDC restrictions on public gatherings. Stimulus packages, unemployment benefits, and free coronavirus tests were all put into motion. Many businesses were closed. Sporting events were cancelled. Buses, trains, and airplanes had to follow the six-foot physical distancing rule, and masks became a requirement.

This pandemic created a worst-case scenario for airlines – even worse than 9/11, after which people stopped flying for a short period of time out of fear. Not only were people concerned about gathering in groups, but the European Union prohibited flights from the US with no clear end date.

When April arrived, American Airlines began asking their employees to voluntarily take paid leaves of absence for anywhere from three months to two years through the Care Act monies they accepted from the government. These leaves included a significantly reduced number of hours – I normally work eighty-five hours a month, and the company was only offering to pay nineteen – so even with the help of unemployment, it was still a huge pay cut. They also offered early retirement packages. At first they were not permitted to furlough any employees because they accepted the government funding, but when the Care Act monies came to an end in September, they once again asked for more volunteers. Their hope was to get enough employees to take leave that the number of furloughs would not be so drastic.

Unfortunately, in this day and age people tend to live beyond their means and not worry about tomorrow, so to speak. It seems like we have created a society that has taught us not to worry about finances because there will always be some kind of bailout – like during the US housing crisis in 2008, when the banks forgave so many loans. As a result, many people are not prepared for this kind of crisis and cannot afford to take leave.

American Airlines has calculated that even with the number of voluntary leaves and retirement packages taken, they will still officially have to lay off 8,120 flight attendants and 1,900 pilots as of October 1, 2020 with no return date in sight. And in this type of situation, bankruptcy is always a possibility. Upon learning about the potential layoffs, a few of our younger flight attendants went and got their real estate license. Others enrolled in culinary school, and some will be moving back into their parents' home to return to university classes, perhaps online. It is highly likely that all these employees will be called back to work eventually, but there is never any guarantee and people are doing what they need to in order to secure a source of income.

Fellow flight attendant Kim Cully shared with me that she "[started] at the age of fifty-five in the midst of a merger, contract negotiations, and uniform poisoning … furloughed at sixty-one." Margaret McCandless Mundy, who has been in the business since 1979, also shared that "9/11 changed my career, 2020 ended my career."

For those who are still working, life isn't easy. We have lost employees to this horrible disease, and being contained in a limited space for hours on end with no fresh air and no possibility of physical distancing is a huge threat to our wellbeing. As my co-worker Julie Forsythe put it, "We are the forgotten essential workers." It is also stressful to see the impacts this pandemic is having on the people you work with and care about; Greg Nevius shares that "I lived through the horror of 9/11. I don't know if I can survive seeing some of my colleagues lose their jobs or lives because of this horrible disease."

After working non-stop for thirty-four years, I volunteered to take a six-month leave of absence from the beginning of May to the end of October. I took this leave for two reasons: to hopefully save someone's job, and to give me an insight as to what retirement might be like. It also was going to become hard for me to get to work – many of the domestic flights to and from Philadelphia, where I am based, have been cancelled – so it's great to have the stress of the commute off my shoulders. I hadn't been overly afraid of catching the virus as we wear a mask and gloves, but I wasn't going to miss dealing with difficult passengers who refused to follow the rules.

I have been off for six months now, and I must tell you that it has been somewhat of an adjustment. I have been lucky that my leave started during the summer here in Pittsburgh, and that has made it lovely. I am very active and can keep busy all day long. I exercise regularly by going on walks and bicycling throughout the city. I have a motorcycle and a three-wheeled T-Rex that I enjoy riding. I have many friends in the city, and we get together on a regular basis. I have been writing quite a bit during this time off – a passion I've been exploring more since becoming a bestselling author – and that has been an exciting project. I have only taken one short trip to Florida during this time because of the pandemic, but all-in-all it's been a relatively nice experience. My fellow flight attendant

Kimberley Waterman shares a similar perspective: "Life in the fast lane was all I knew and wanted, but after taking the three-month leave, I found a new appreciation for flowers, squirrels, and shopping."

What's really strange to me is that although I have not gained an ounce during my leave, I have noticed a shift in my body weight. Pulling a suitcase, running from plane to plane, lifting luggage in and out of the cars and overhead compartments, running to the vans to get to the hotels, and constantly standing are all forms of exercise we just never seem to count.

The company has asked for more volunteers to take leave, as well as asking those of us who are already on a leave to take an extension. I have elected to take an additional six months because I am able and willing to do so, which will bring me to June 2021. I am somewhat nervous about getting through the winter months – although I am an avid snowboarder, I won't be able to walk out the front door and enjoy the weather as I do right now. I also know in my heart that I am not ready for retirement. It is not the lifestyle that I want right now. Perhaps those who have not enjoyed their work are eager to get out and explore a different way of living and are counting the days to their retirement, but not me. I miss the busyness of it all, the people, and of course the international overnight trips. I miss my salted butter from Paris, my olive oils from Lisbon, and my wines from Rome. I will be eager to get back to work in June, and I hope that my international routes will be there waiting for me and this disease will be under control.

The pandemic has put a lot of people and businesses into dire financial needs, and for many this was out of their control. But for some, putting a bit more effort into maintaining their finances throughout their life would have put them in a much better position to handle this sort of crisis. And thankfully, it is never too late to start.

I tell my nephew – as my mother told me – go out and see the world, enjoy life, be curious, and take risks, but always know the importance of being financially and mentally able to handle these adventures. This means look ahead, have somewhat of a plan, build a savings account, live within your means, and be patient with life. There is always time to achieve your goals, little by little. Have no fear and take advantage of opportunities that come your way. Build your resume and have big dreams. Go for it – all of it. Don't be shy about making mistakes, but make sure you learn from them. Enjoy every moment of this learning experience, and you will only reap benefits.

About Helen (Chome) Horwat

Helen was born in Brownsville, PA in 1953. She went on to become a recruiter for the US Information Agency in Washington, DC and then became a certified expert examiner through the State Department. She also trained as a graphic artist and was privileged to work on the *America Illustrated Russian Magazine*, which is now a part of the John Marsh Files at the Gerald R. Ford Presidential Library.

Helen became a model with the Ford Modeling Agency in NYC in 1977 and later opened her own state-licensed modeling school, Finesse. She also became a lecturer and motivational speaker on the topics of dressing for success, job interviewing techniques, and promoting yourself through your resume.

In her personal life, Helen raised her nephew from the age of six and was the caregiver for both of her parents in their final years. She has spent the last thirty-three years working for American Airlines as a flight attendant, enabling her to do what she enjoys most: travel the world and be there for her passengers. She has become a bestselling author through the WOW book *Aging at Any Age with Moxie!* and is now writing her autobiography.

Email: chomehorwat@mac.com

9

Do It Afraid

by Christine Mack

"To feel fear doesn't mean that you're a coward. Boldness is taking action in the presence of fear — do it afraid!"
Joyce Meyer

Do It Afraid

By Christine Mack

I have always felt that I had to do things the hard way. Nothing ever came easily for me, and there were many challenges that I have had to overcome. I completed my Licensed Practical Nurse program in 2009 with four children all under the age of four (I welcomed my fifth child shortly after). It was the toughest year of my life, but I was determined to get it done. I was dedicated and studied hard, and I completed it with the support of my family. My husband and I separated three years ago, so we are sharing custody of our children and I am juggling life as a single mother. I also struggled with an addiction to alcohol for many years, but I overcame it and have been sober since January 13, 2018. And now, I have decided to go back to school and pursue my Bachelor of Science in Nursing to further my career.

I was going through my first year of university when the pandemic hit – thankfully, I was about ninety percent done with my courses and was able to finish them online. As soon as they were over, I went right back into the workforce as an LPN at a long-term care facility.

I have held this position for eleven years, but when I returned things looked a lot different than what I was used to. Our facility had gone into lockdown as per Dr. Bonnie Henry's order. Visitors were not allowed to enter; the residents were not allowed to leave, with the exception of going to medical appointments or to the hospital. We had one assigned doctor who came to the facility once a week, so we had to prioritize who needed to be seen. We took the residents' temperatures twice a day and monitored their health closely. Staff were only permitted to work at one facility to prevent the spread of the virus – if you usually worked at more that one building, you had to pick one and stick with it. We had to bring our uniforms to work and change in a designated area, and we left our street clothing there throughout our shift. We then had to go through a screening desk where we were asked about our health or any possible symptoms. Our temperatures were taken and we were given a mask to wear. At the end of the day, we had to get our temperature taken again and then change out of our uniform, and leave out of a designated door.

These precautions were necessary to protect the vulnerable population we served, but they came with their own problems. I noticed an overall decline in the mental health of the residents, the majority of whom have dementia. They did not understand what was going on; all they knew was that they were cut off from their spouse or their families. We explained the current situation to them, but they would often forget. We did our best to keep them happy and content, with the staff spending extra time doing activities or puzzles or playing board games. Unfortunately, there was only so much we could do.

After three months, families were finally allowed to come back in so long as they wore gowns and a mask. While this was a great relief to many, some residents could not even recognize their own family under all the protective gear.

By the summer of 2020, I was overwhelmed. The weight of everything was becoming so heavy that I felt like I was falling apart. My work was extremely stressful, and there was so much going on in my family life. One night, I reached my breaking point. I felt like I was doing all this work for nothing, and I was ready to give up. I did not want to feel this way anymore. I wanted to escape my reality and fall into my addictions again. I went to bed with a very heavy heart and prayed to God for peace – peace in my life, and peace in my heart.

When I woke up the next morning, I came across a video on Facebook that caught my eye. A lady was sharing her testimony about how the gap between her and God had widened. She had spoken to God, and he had told her that he was always there, and to just trust and have faith. I felt like this was a message also meant for me – a reminder to have faith. I cried and prayed, and I felt the weight I had been carrying lift from my shoulders. Knowing that I wasn't alone gave me so much strength.

I am grateful that I did not fall back into my addictions. Becoming sober took so much strength and dedication, and I have worked hard to get where I am in life. I have had to let go of shame and guilt. I had to forgive myself and forgive others who have hurt me. I have had to learn some tools to help navigate this road. I created this life that I am living. The pandemic certainly threatened my sobriety – the consistent state of panic and stress that came with the shutdowns and isolation were especially challenging for people dealing with addictions. But I have done my best to keep my mind healthy. I listen to a lot of podcasts – my favourites are Tony Robbins, Brené Brown, and Lisa Nichols. I also continue to attend meetings to assist with my recovery.

While the pandemic presented me with new obstacles to overcome, it also provided me with the opportunity to learn what truly was important to me and grow as a person. This has changed me in so many ways. For one, my relationship with my children's father has improved, and we are now able to co-parent in a more effective and loving way. When we first broke up, we could only communicate by email. I had a lot of anger, so I was not very respectful in the way I spoke with him and our conversations always became an argument. It took a couple years for me to let go of the hurt and anger I was feeling and learn to respond rather than react – this was not an easy process for me. During the pandemic, though, I learned what really mattered to me, and that was my family. I just wanted everyone to be safe, happy, and healthy. This helped us to work together as a team to ensure our children were safe. We were even able to put our differences aside and go on our first outing as a family to a nearby lake. It was a breath of fresh air, and our children are happier for it.

My relationship with my children has also improved during this time. Prior to the pandemic, I felt like I was running from the moment I woke up to the moment my head hit the pillow at night. I took every opportunity I could to spend time with my family and close friends, but those opportunities were few and far between. Once the shutdowns arrived and there was nowhere to go, my kids and I got to have more quality time together. We spent a lot of our time going to lakes and hiking in and around Kamloops, and we made so many beautiful memories. My son told me that one of his best memories is when we ordered pizza and had a dance party outdoors. I am grateful for having this time with them, and I will always hold these memories close to my heart.

Another major thing that changed for me during the pandemic was that I spent some time truly alone for the first time since my children were born. Because I am a front-line worker, the kids went to their dad's for almost two weeks – we both felt this was the safest option because we had some significant concerns about me bringing home the virus. This was one of the longest times that I had been alone, and it forced me to recognize how my past traumas had affected me. I had abandonment issues that I had not been fully aware of, but now I was forced to sit still long enough to deal with them. It was uncomfortable and awkward. I kept in touch with my counsellor to help me deal with this, and I did some online courses to help me better understand myself. One perspective that really stood out to me is that when you are a child, you are abandoned, but when you are an adult, people simply leave. I used to be so afraid of change, and I would cry if anyone would move away or leave.

Getting through this time spent by myself has made me stronger. I had to let myself feel that uncomfortable silence so I could learn about myself, and I had to deal with the feelings that arose in a productive way. As a result, I am now better able to cope with my emotions and find healthy ways of dealing with them.

This pandemic has also reinforced one of the greatest lessons that I have learned so far in my life, and that is to "just do it afraid." Nothing grows in your comfort zone; in order to move forward in life, you have to be willing to face your fear, feel it, and overcome it. This concept has helped me with many of my decisions in the past three years. Even when I first told my family that I wanted to go back to school, I felt like I was standing on the edge of the cliff getting ready to jump. Not only was I going to be a "starving student," but I was also taking my five children with me. These are the moments that define us. As scared as I was that day, I still took the leap and am better for it.

As I write this chapter, I am getting prepared to go back to university. Part of me wanted to put my dream on hold for a year because I have a lot to juggle as a single mother. My five children will all be in different schools, and I know that managing this during a pandemic will be remarkably busy. However, I was finally able to obtain full sponsorship for my schooling which includes tuition, books, and a living allowance to ensure I am successful in my studies. I've worked hard to get to this point, and there is no turning back now.

The world is filled with so much panic and fear, but personally, I feel more inner peace than I've ever felt before. I have grown so much. I have learned so much. I have let go of so much. I have changed so much. I will choose to take these positive changes and use them to keep moving forward. I will continue to face my fear and do it afraid, and I am excited to see where this journey will take me.

About Christine Mack

Christine is from the Nuxalk Nation in Bella Coola, BC (the heart of the Great Bear Rainforest). Before smallpox ravaged the area, there were 200 communities; after smallpox, less than 200 people survived. They all came together, and this is how Bella Coola was formed. As a result, resiliency is in Christine's blood. She takes pride in being a strong Nuxalk woman and mother to her five beautiful children. Her children have given her the strength she needed to continue moving forward and start her healing journey.

Christine began her career in healthcare in 2002. She started as a Resident Care Aide and then furthered her education to become a Licensed Practical Nurse in 2008. She has been an LPN since 2009 and spent all these years working in dementia care at various nursing homes in Kamloops, BC.

Christine has plans to further her education and become a Registered Nurse. Having a child with mental health problems and losing both her best friends to addictions has made her passionate about mental health and addictions. She is going to pursue that path and plans to work in mental health and/or addictions after she has completed the Registered Nurse program.

Email: christinef81@outlook.com

10

Mental Health Vital Signs

by Alyson Jones MA, RCC and Jacqueline Fowler BSN, MD

"Resiliency is the intersection of strength and vulnerability. This is the place where we ultimately embrace all aspects of our humanity and the humanity of others. "

Alyson Jones and Jacqueline Fowler

Mental Health Vital Signs

By Alyson Jones MA, RCC
and Jacqueline Fowler BSN, MD

Terry sent Alyson an email to ask for an emergency Zoom counselling session as she was having a very bad day. Terry is forty-four, married, and has two young children. She works in the financial services industry – her office used to be downtown, but now she is working out of the small extra room in her home. Terry is not a dramatic person, so her request for an emergency session made it clear she was having a tough time. Alyson responded that she could make herself available and added Terry onto the end of her clinical day.

At 5:00 p.m., Alyson sent out the Zoom link. There was a bit of a technological glitch at the beginning, but after some momentary panic they got things working and the call started, albeit a bit late. When they finally settled into the session, Terry burst into tears and said, "I just can't take it anymore. I hate this virus and I just want life to be like it used to be." Alyson helped Terry through her tears, and together they practiced some mindful breathing. She went on to say, "I can't keep up with all of this. I feel stressed all the time. I feel like I have to figure things out all the time. My husband and I have been arguing. I cannot keep up to the changing rules. Are we all supposed to wear masks now when we are out in public? I am always telling my children to social distance and wear a mask, but they do not really listen to me anymore. I don't really know who is in my bubble and who is not." Terry was overwhelmed.

Alyson did some grounding exercises with her and unbundled some of the challenges she was experiencing. She also reassured Terry that it was normal for her to be feeling this way. After letting off some steam and receiving validation, Terry had a self-care plan in place for the next week and said she felt much better.

Alyson got off the Zoom call at 6:15 p.m. and realized she had not moved her body for three hours straight. These sorts of sessions are not the exception in her counselling practice anymore – they are the norm and occur almost daily.

The struggles Terry was facing have become a part of our collective experience. The year 2020 will stand out as the year that changed how we approach not just public health, but also our way of life. The pandemic brought the world to a standstill – odd images of empty streets in some of the largest and busiest cities are fresh in our minds. This virus also changed our global narrative on health in only a matter of months. Through social media and technology, we heard and saw how the pandemic was playing out around the world. The stories of hospitals overflowing and not having enough supplies became a reality in far too many places. The numbers of cases have been staggering, and we know we are not through it yet.

This pandemic has not just been a medical crisis, it has been a mental health pandemic as well. It has delivered significant amounts of anxiety, depression, and stress along with the physical health concerns.

A Mental Health Pandemic – Alyson

We have been having a global conversation on how to deal with this pandemic, which has increased everyone's awareness of medical guidelines. Who could have predicted that infectious disease protocols would become part of our everyday conversations? We must wash our hands like a doctor, avoid touching our face, and disinfect common surfaces to the best of our ability. When we leave home, we take our hand sanitizer and face masks with us. Now the next wave of conversations has begun, and it is about minding our mental health in this new age.

In our contribution to book five in the Woman Of Worth book series, Mental Health Matters, Dr. Jacqueline Fowler and I introduced the concept that mental health IS health. With over fifty years of combined experience in the medical and mental health fields, we addressed the stigmatization of mental health issues. I am a child and family therapist, a registered clinical counsellor, and the clinical director of Alyson Jones & Associates. Jacqueline Fowler is a family physician and former registered nurse who has worked with thousands of patients. Our combined commitment is to enhance health and healing through increased awareness around how mental health is part of our overall health.

Mental health and physical health are not two different

concepts, but rather different parts of the same conversation. However, while people are often supportive and sympathetic to a person who is suffering from a physical challenge, this support has not always extended to mental health challenges. Jacqueline and I strongly believe that an integrated approach to physical and mental health is the best way forward for all of humanity, especially as we deal with this pandemic.

The United Nations and the World Health Organization have identified that mental health is a serious global concern at this time. We need strategies and protocols to help deepen our understanding and response to mental health issues. There are many factors that impact stress levels, including support systems, community, finances, and past health concerns. Fear of exposure to the virus is also a significant stressor. It is natural to feel stress, anxiety, and grief during this pandemic – in fact, not experiencing some of these would be unusual.

There have been significant changes to our routines and activities as a result of this virus. Social distancing can help limit transmission, but it can also leave people feeling lonely and isolated. As a therapist, I have seen my clients struggle with overwhelm, fear, anxiety, and feeling isolated in their own homes. Personally, I have struggled with this in my own life. I am a social person and have always enjoyed seeing my clients face-to-face as well as attending events and trainings to enhance my practice. With the advent of social distancing, these activities were now limited to a computer screen.

When the pandemic first hit, I realized I was going to have to see my clients virtually rather than in person. This involved an incredible amount of learning and daily adaptations. It took a lot of time, energy, and problem-solving to transition myself, my office, my associates, and my clients to an online format. As much as I am grateful for Zoom and other electronic platforms, the learning curve and the constant screen time was exhausting. My practice now has a combination of both online and in-person sessions, and it is great to have these options. But the reality still remains that I am on my computer much more than I used to be. After a full day of virtual meetings and sessions, that last thing I want to do is have a social Zoom with my friends. We all appreciate being able to connect electronically, but this does not replace seeing each other in person. Too much screen time can leave us feeling stressed and alone.

This pandemic has created uncertainty and threatened life as we know it. For some, it has threatened their very lives. We are faced with the new realities of working from home, an increased dependence on technology, changes in education, a fear of exposure, and a lack of physical contact with others. It is normal and understandable that we are experiencing a mental health pandemic along with the physical one.

A Medical and Mental Health Perspective – Jacqueline

Our mental health is an important part of our overall health and wellbeing. It affects how we think, feel, and act. It also impacts our physical health, how we handle stress, how we relate to others, and how we make choices. Mental health issues may be acute and associated with some of the short-term stressors this pandemic has brought. However, people with pre-existing mental health conditions are particularly vulnerable right now and are likely to be adversely impacted by the current world situation. Therefore, it is important for these people to stay in contact with their health providers – both physical and mental – during these challenging times to monitor any new or worsening symptoms. For those with emerging issues, it is also important to reach out and seek assistance sooner rather than later so that treatment can be implemented quickly to prevent more serious complications from arising.

We can manage our mental health by using practical information in the same manner that doctors do when they are assessing the health of an individual. Medical health professionals use vital signs – physical indicators that provide information about a person's condition – as a tool to assess and monitor a patient. Examples of medical vital signs include temperature, heart rate, blood pressure, and respiratory rate. When one or more of these is not behaving as expected, the observer can quickly use this to gain valuable information.

Here is an example of how vital signs can be an important part of healthcare. Judy had been a patient at my family practice for five years. She was a healthy young woman and did not have any significant pre-existing conditions. One day, she arrived at my office feeling worried and perplexed. "Doc, I'm just not feeling good," she says. A quick check of her vital signs revealed an elevated heart rate and respiratory rate – this is unusual for a thirty-five-year-old woman at rest. Thinking about a number of possible explanations, I asked her, "Any chest pain or shortness of breath?" She stopped and said, "Well, come to think of it … yes." This information, along with her vital signs, lead me to wonder if she might be experiencing some serious complications from an oral contraceptive she was on. I sent her to emergency for additional tests, and it was soon discovered that she had a pulmonary embolism. She was admitted to hospital and was treated successfully for this potentially fatal condition. If I had not checked her vital signs, this complication could have been missed.

Vital signs help us to identify a problem so that we can provide the appropriate treatment. Similarly, mental health vital signs can be an effective tool to quickly obtain information regarding an individual's state of mental wellbeing. Here are some of the signs of mental distress that may need further investigation:

- Difficulty concentrating and making decisions
- Changes in appetite, energy, and activity levels
- Increased emotional reactivity
- Difficulty sleeping or troubled dreams
- Somatic changes (headaches, body pains, stomach problems)
- Worsening of chronic physical and mental health problems
- Increased use of substances

One does not have to be a doctor or therapist to pay attention to the mental health vital signs of the people around you. If you suspect that someone is in psychological distress, Alyson and I have developed a mental health tool that can be used to help assess a person's mental health and determine whether professional intervention might be warranted.

The Mental Health Vital Signs Checklist

Below is a quick and easy tool you can use on yourself or others. There are ten mental health vital signs, and each has a maximum score of five, which would indicate there is no problem or concern in that area. The highest you can get on the whole checklist is fifty. The higher you score, the better your vital signs; the lower the score, the more you may be struggling. A score of twenty-five or lower indicates that a check-in with your health and mental health providers might be warranted.

The Mental Health Vital Signs Checklist (Developed by Alyson Jones & Dr. Jacqueline Fowler)

Vital Sign	1 Very Poor	2 Poor	3 Neutral	4 Good	5 Excellent/ No problem	Score
Sleep Pattern						
Concentration Level						
Social Support						
Overall Mood						
Level of Worry/Stress						
Appetite						
Activity and Energy Level						
Substance Use and Abuse						
Self Harming Behaviours or Thoughts						
Life Stressors						
Overall Score						

Copyright Jones/Fowler. Redistribution, reuse, and adaption permitted and subject to attribution of the original text copyright holders.

If you or someone you care about is scoring low on the Mental Health Vital Signs Checklist, there are actions you can take. You can speak up and share your concerns, offer support and assistance, and encourage the person to reach out to their health and mental health care providers. Also, one of the most important things you can do to support someone is to keep checking in and keep the conversation going. As a global community, we united to respond to the public health crisis we are facing. In the same vein, we need to unite as a community to support each other's mental wellbeing.

Creating Resiliency

Humans are amazingly resilient. Every one of us will have experienced some sort of physical and emotional suffering throughout our lives, and yet we keep adapting to the challenges in front of us. Although this pandemic is big and daunting, it is also an opportunity to bounce back and experience growth. The Chinese word for crisis has two symbols: one for danger and one for opportunity. This is a fitting description for the reality we now find ourselves in – although there are dangers in this pandemic, there are also opportunities.

As we work on embracing the changes in our lives, there are things we can do to protect our mental health in the process. Here are ten tips for minding your mental health and building resiliency in this new age:

1. **Keep checking in with each other.** Ask questions, listen, and do your best to be empathetic and understanding of what others are experiencing. People will share as much or as little as they are comfortable with.
2. **Keep it real.** We will have good days and bad days. In fact, we might even have good hours and bad hours within a day. We will swing back and forth between gratitude and frustration.
3. **Do not beat yourself up – you cannot be everything to everyone all the time!** If your day feels like a failure, just recognize that it was one of "those" days. You cannot be a top producer at work, fitness guru, gourmet chef, and

super schoolteacher all day every day. You are human, and that is what we like about you!

4. **Expect frustrations and admit your own bad moods.** No matter how much we want to handle things with grace, the reality is there will be times when we do not. Let go of your ego and do not waste time on defensiveness. If you have been irritable or unpleasant, admit it. Try to get over yourself as quickly as possible and say sorry – and mean it.

5. **Be forgiving and kind.** Forgive yourself for your own frustrations and forgive others for theirs. In essence, be kind to each other. When we work through something, we build more intimacy and resiliency in our relationships.

6. **Keep a sense of humour.** It is good for us to laugh at ourselves and the absurdities in life. Who knew toilet paper could be so funny and make such great memes! Laughter is essential to good mental health and an important part of resiliency. A good laugh can be our saving grace.

7. **Find Support Groups.** Find like-minded people in similar situations – you can do this electronically or while social distancing. It is important to commiserate with others and share the emotional load.

8. **Stay informed but know when to back off from the news.** When you feel that you are missing information, gather what you need – but also take breaks from watching, reading, or listening to news stories when you become overwhelmed.

9. **Have a routine but expect disruptions.** Humans need structure, and our brains like patterns. Make sure you are giving your brain predictable routines and patterns

to thrive within. Set up a schedule, and then be prepared to be flexible and allow the rest to flow.

10. **Take some private time inside and outside.** We all need time together, but we also need time alone. It is okay to let others know when you just need some "me-time." Explore some of your interests or just chill with a good book or a show. Get some daily oxygen intake. If you have a garden, yard, or balcony, go out on it! If you have a window, open it. Go for walks. Breathe, and breathe in deeply. Focus on your senses as you connect with the great outdoors.

We are grateful that you took the time to read this chapter, and encourage you to travel along with us as we move forward and lead others in developing a greater understanding of mental health and wellness. Life is complex, and we all struggle along the way. By taking steps to improve our resiliency, checking in with our vital signs, and reaching out when we notice an issue developing, we can support our health from all angles. And remember, mental health IS health!

About the Authors

Jacqueline Fowler, BSN, MD has spent more than thirty years working in the healthcare field, first as a nurse and then as a doctor. She has taken a special interest in assisting those with mental illness and their support systems. She strives to share her expertise and enjoys contributing to a deeper understanding of health, mental health, and resiliency. Jacqueline is also the mother of two young adults.

Alyson Jones, MA, RCC is a professional therapist and mental health educator as well as the president of a large private counselling clinic, Alyson Jones & Associates. She holds a Master's degree in psychology and has practiced for over twenty-five years, working with all age groups. Alyson is prominent in the psychological community and is often invited by the media to share her extensive knowledge on mental health, parenting, children, and families. She is a regular on CTV Morning Live and a contributing writer to Slica.ca and Huffington Post.

www.alysonjones.ca
LinkedIn: Alyson Jones
Facebook: Alyson Jones & Associates
Twitter: @MOREalysonjones
Instagram: @alysonjonesassociates

Together, Alyson and Jackie have originated the YouTube channel "Master Your Mental Health" to provide mental health tips to viewers.

YouTube:
www.youtube.com/channel/UC-K2Zpp8cgN3iaszSRBatEg
Email: masteryourmentalhealth@gmail.com

11

Be the Difference

by Corisa Bell

"To be yourself in a world that is constantly trying to make you something else is the greatest accomplishment."
Ralph Waldo Emerson

Be the Difference

By Corisa Bell

The pandemic arrived at a time when I was already in the midst of extreme chaos. Over the past year, the beautiful future I had thought I was building with my life partner had been slowly revealing itself to be a fictitious nightmare. When I first met my partner, I truly thought I'd met my prince charming. We were like two peas in a pod, bonding and making jokes about how the saying "it's too good to be true" didn't apply to us. It was too perfect; I later learned this is a tactic called "mirroring" that covert narcissists use to project an image of being the perfect mate. He was the first to say "I love you." He said he had never wanted to propose to a woman before me and yet couldn't stop talking about how he was going to marry me one day. He made me feel special and treated me the way I had always felt a woman deserved to be treated.

Everything seemed so dreamy – at least for awhile.

The longer I spent with him, the more I could sense his words and stories were actually lies. However, I have Complex PTSD and he would use this to manipulate me, causing me to become so confused as to what was reality and what wasn't. I was caught in a game I didn't even know I was playing – this is the power of gaslighting. He said the inconsistencies in our relationship were my fault, not his, and I even started to believe him.

Ironically, as part of the undergraduate degree I am currently working toward, I started a course in January 2020 which included studying psychopaths and other behaviour disorders. As my course progressed, it became clear that the words on the pages of my textbook described the reality I was living. And as I put together the puzzle pieces and created timelines, I began to realize this wasn't only my story. I reached out to other women I suspected had gone through the same experience and began understanding so much more about who this man actually was.

It was through connecting with these other women that I learned how powerful it is to have the perspectives of others available to me so that I can put together the entire truth. Reaching out provided all of us a safe place to heal because we had more information together than we ever could have had during our individual experiences with him. We were able to confirm that his behaviours and sentiments were literally copied and pasted from one of us to the next. We took comfort in being able to know for certain that we weren't to blame for his actions, and because of this we were able to make an impossible situation better. The other women provided me the certainty and strength I needed to stand up for myself, expose him, and confidently leave the relationship.

This situation highlighted how important it is to have all the information before reaching conclusions. If I had just left this relationship believing there was something wrong with me because he said so, then I would've carried that with me for who knows how many years and things never would have made sense. It wouldn't have been possible to understand things the way I did now if it weren't for the shared knowledge I received from others.

I was in the process of piecing myself back together when it was announced school would not resume at the end of spring break. This really got my attention; something serious was happening. I had to lift myself out of rawness in order to enter into action mode. In this sense, the pandemic was a personal blessing. I had to let go of what happened and focus on things that were much bigger than me. I was able to step out of the CPTSD loop of repeatedly retracing each intricacy of the last year of my life and step into the present. I was completely numb, but I could hold onto and take with me the beauty of humanity because of the lovely women that had been there to express compassion and build each other up. Feeling this gave me hope that society could also come together to thrive during this challenging time.

As I first examined the response to the pandemic, I was grateful to see so many people engaged in a global conversation. I had never seen anything like it. This was the first time I had been able to really understand how people around the entire world processed information, how they responded to a crisis, and how different governments reacted to a significant event that would affect the collective. It was like all of a sudden there was a level of transparency we'd never before experienced in society, and with my own political experience I knew it was just as important to read between the lines as it was to read the lines we were given.

As the days went by, though, the majority of people seemed to be blindly accepting the narratives presented in social media and defending these ideals and platforms without being fully and globally informed. Many weren't making an effort to get all the information, something I was especially disappointed to see from my friends – particularly the people in a position of power who were in a place to create a real conversation.

Concerned with this blind acceptance of a mainstream narrative, I encouraged people to do their own research and to look into the opinions of other doctors, not just the information provided by the WHO, the CDC, and the appointed public health officials. I stressed the importance of being informed from all sides and angles of the political conversations that were taking place in each country, which then would provide further clarity about the pandemic conversation. In response, I was receiving quite aggressive reactions, which in turn created fear within myself about the future of democracy as we knew it.

At this time, I felt the responsible thing to do was a check-in with myself to see how I was personally processing and filtering information. As someone who has been diagnosed with Complex PTSD and therefore needs to carefully manage potential threats, I needed to know for certain if the fear I was experiencing was truly due to my disappointment in others or if it was my own fear response that was going to lead me down a path that could cause me to be unhealthy. I had to hold my own hand and be my own best friend as I continued down the hundreds of rabbit holes seeking truth, researching global politics, and learning about public health. The more that I researched, the more concerned I became that we were moving towards a complete dependency on government, and that this would have a significant negative impact on our future rights and freedoms.

I tried to share what I was finding on social media. I expressed repeatedly that I wasn't sharing information to tell people what to think, but rather was wanting the things I posted to encourage and inspire others to do their own research. I wanted to encourage us all to look beyond what we were being told – to reach out to other humans in other countries and share our knowledge so that we could get as close as we could to the whole truth. Even though I was starting to get messages and phone calls from others who were now seeing what I had been seeing, publicly I was still met with so much resistance to anything that didn't fit into the mainstream narrative.

I understood then, as I do now, that part of the issue is that we've been institutionally conditioned to not be critical thinkers. I know social media is only free because it's designed to collect information in a plethora of ways, which is then used to market certain products to us. I know that algorithms are also used to control what we're being exposed to,

real or not, by showing us news from specific sources. Through this, these platforms can have an incredible influence on our thoughts and beliefs. This is also detrimental to critical thinking as it creates an echo chamber where we never have to question our opinions because we're only offered information that backs up what we already believe. In this era of misinformation, one has to work very hard to be able to piece together the entire truth.

Even though it is our own perceptions that create our reality, with every keystroke our individual psyches are being documented and people are paying for this collected information 24/7. This tool is then capitalized on to influence what we believe in, what we purchase, and even how we vote.

This is one of the reasons that having knowledge about something doesn't automatically make it true. It's important to be collectors of information so that when a situation arises, we have plenty of information to understand the underlying agendas at play. We can either choose to evolve through shared knowledge and discussions, learning together as a society by receiving all types of information before reaching a conclusion, or we can stay with the same thinking we've always had and potentially be unprepared for the future ahead. I believe it's my inherent responsibility to keep educated on issues around the world that will not only affect my own family but will also shape the future they inherit. I feel it is healthy to challenge our belief systems and sift through everything that we're being told to make sure the world we live in continues to be trustworthy and in the best interest of all people, not only a few.

While I was dealing with the negativity and hostility I was receiving from people, I was also witnessing political agendas being achieved across the globe and trying to prevent myself from being sent into a spiral of fear as I was no longer feeling safe. Being in charge of CPTSD means managing triggers before they happen, and a big trigger for me is living in a false reality as this is where the abuse I've experienced takes place. I know that I am the only person in charge of my body, mind, and health, but I still have to convince and remind myself that I'm equipped to handle the unknown. This is an ongoing relationship with myself. Information is my personal safety net, but I had to respectfully understand most people weren't obsessed with information the same way I was. To me, information is a symbol of life or death. To me, information is a symbol of either a democracy or a dictatorship.

In between all my research (I stopped counting at five-hundred hours), self-reflection, and decision-making, there were many times when I needed to step away from it all, breathe, and soak in all that I find beautiful. I needed to balance the negativity I was taking in with positivity as much as possible, as the information I was consuming in mass quantities was consistently triggering my fear response.

It has been through the diagnosis of CPTSD I've become closely acquainted with emotional intelligence. I drew on these lessons and constantly reconfirmed what I was responsible for and what I was in control of. I did this because when something within us isn't centered, our feelings become uncomfortable. This is our soul's way of communicating that something needs to be tended to, just like aches and pains do for our physical body. And just like a physical injury, an emotional injury can become even more damaging if not resolved in the immediate. I understood that if I didn't let go of these emotional injuries my fear was creating, then it would take longer for me to feel that I was still in fact in charge of myself. I reminded myself how important it is to listen to myself, to breath, and to take the time I needed to process my environmental intake and truly filter everything through my emotions so I didn't hold onto the negativity. I took a close look at what I am responsible for and what solutions I am capable of. When I do this, I can clearly see what concepts I'm personally taking on that I actually have zero direct control over. I am also reminded that I am solely responsible for how I react to everything around me.

After going through this process, I came to the conclusion that the basis of everything that is me is the desire to be there for others. I needed to take a step away from the nastiness of politics, surround myself in positivity and the light of God, and just be with people, for people. I prayed with God consistently to let me use my abilities to help people know they were loved. I wanted to make people happy and alleviate their concerns, fears, and pain. The next thing I knew, I received a phone call about a position that was exactly what I was looking for. Within two weeks I was a community builder for a major non-profit, spreading love like wildfire! Constantly staying in touch with who I was, how I was processing things, and what I needed not only kept me healthy through these last six months, but also allowed me to be open to opportunity when it came because I already knew what I wanted and had directly asked for it. Energy only speaks in the language of what you are asking for; it doesn't understand conflicting messages.

As we continue to make our way through this pandemic, I feel we need to pay attention to what we want our world to look like at the end of it. Everyone – every single one of us – creates the reality we live in. I feel strongly that we cannot truly be a part of progress if we don't have a solid understanding of the history and circumstances that led us to the current collective direction, and we can only do this by truly being authentic to ourselves during our internal processing of external circumstances. We must inform ourselves and make decisions that allow us to breathe and feel passionate about the lives we're living, and we must support those around us – especially the ones we love – to do the same. This may mean letting go of a person who does not lift us up, changing the amount of energy we put into something, or perhaps doing something entirely different. We should feel like we're skating through life, growing stronger with each decision we make. Doing this will naturally benefit the world and those around us because we will give off an energy of love, healing, and positivity as opposed to confusion, uncertainty, and negativity.

To achieve this, we need to know ourselves so well that we understand why we are the way we are. We need to know how we respond to the world as we perceive it. We must constantly be evolving and striving for who we want to be and what we want our world to look like; otherwise, we are settling for letting outside influences define our very existence. As we age and collect new experiences and information, we need to be re-examining these aspects of ourselves over and over throughout our entire lives and continually open ourselves up to new ideas, new ways of seeing things, and opportunities for self-evolution. We need to let go of parts of who we were so that we can become who we are now. Leaving parts of ourselves behind can be hard, but it's not sad. Being fluid in a complicated world is how we can live the fullest life possible. It is how we grow.

I truly believe we can heal the world, one life at a time. However, unless something directly affects us, we aren't usually motivated to do something about it. In this way, the pandemic is a blessing for us all. Things are not as they should be right now, but this disruption is necessary for great improvement. There must be chaos before the calmness, and then reinvention can settle in. The world is adjusting in the biggest way, and so should we. We must speak our truths as loud as the truth that is currently getting the most attention; if we aren't voicing our beliefs and realities, the world will only be designed by those who are taking action and voicing theirs.

At the end of the day, there are two questions we must ask ourselves: who we want to be, and how we want to be remembered. Our children will end up much like us, no matter how much effort we put into telling them to be different, so we must think about modelling how we want our children to be in this complicated world as well. Don't expect the difference, be the difference.

About Corisa Bell

Corisa Bell is enthusiastic about everything she undertakes. After partnering in a successful e-commerce software development company, she served two terms in local government and sat twice as president of the Lower Mainland Local Government Association. Currently retired from political life, she enjoys public speaking, selective consultant work, and is about to retire as vice president of the local Chamber of Commerce. She works part time as a community builder for a major non-profit, is a full-time philosophy student at UFV, and spends her spare time out in nature or volunteering for various boards and societies.

As a young person, Corisa had fallen through the cracks; because of this personal experience, her passion is being there for people and letting them know they aren't alone and that they're loved. To fulfill this passion, she currently serves on the boards for Camp Choice BC and the Christmas Haven.

Corisa loves the two beautiful souls she proudly calls her daughters, Rhyly and Kaylyn. She has raised her girls to think of their community as their extended family, and she is in her happy place when with community.

www.campchoicebc.com
www.christmashaven.ca
Email: corisabell@gmail.com

12

Passion Through a Pandemic

by Karen Kobel

"My mission in life is not to survive, but to thrive; and to do so with passion, some compassion, some humor, and some style."
Maya Angelou

Passion Through a Pandemic

By Karen Kobel

Throughout my life, there are three passions that I have pursued: movement, dance, and bringing people together. Following these desires brought me to a career as a dancer, which then blossomed into teaching dance, Pilates, and yoga. While turning these passions into my life's work hasn't always been easy, I have pushed forward with positivity and persistence to grow myself and my teaching practice, eventually achieving my dream of opening my own studio in April 2017.

Kahlena Movement Studio – located in North Vancouver, BC – is a welcoming place where people of all levels can come together to explore, grow, and laugh. On top of the regular Pilates, yoga, and dance classes, we offer prenatal and postnatal classes, parent and toddler, kids dance, workshops for movement and meditation, educational and emotional learning for kids, full moon ceremonies, women's circles, and "shop local" pop-up events. My vision has always been based on building community and holding space for others to come and feel the energy, love, and kindness we have created within these walls. We celebrate your victories and encourage you in moments of doubt, providing a supportive space where you can build your exercise regime one class at a time.

At the beginning of March 2020, we were getting ready to sign a five-year lease for our studio space and to keep the business growing. However, as the anxiety and curiosity around the pandemic grew, there was some inclination that a shutdown was coming. We all knew things were about to change – if not forever, then at least for our immediate future. On March 16, I arrived at the studio and realized that no one had pre-registered for my class, which in previous weeks had thirteen clients in attendance. I looked at the mountain view outside, closed my eyes, took a deep breath, and felt a tear roll down my cheek. I was about to make one of the hardest business decisions to date: to close our doors without knowing for how long.

As I stood there, I took a second to mourn the loss of our in-person classes. There are so many benefits to coming into the studio for your Pilates, yoga, dance, and fitness classes. The instructor can watch your alignment, see your posture and what needs to be adjusted, observe your movements three-dimensionally, and connect the posture adjustments to the movement adjustments. There is an energy transfer that happens from teacher to client, and from client to teacher. Throughout every class, there is this beautiful energy in the room of warmth, support, and love. Also, it is important for us all to have some kind of connection in our day that helps us feel loved and supported. We are creatures who need social interaction, even if that interaction is simply being on your mat next to someone and not necessarily talking. Nothing can replicate this experience.

Unfortunately, in-person classes were completely off the table for the foreseeable future, so I had no other choice but to figure out how to keep our community growing and keep the movement happening. I had to persist and find a new way to push through and pursue my passion. I needed to take Kahlena to the next level: ONLINE. With this new resolve, I opened my eyes and got to work.

Moving to a virtual format was no small task. There was an explosion of online workouts being offered, and many people were giving them away for free. Competition was high, so I had to make sure that my clients were getting what they wanted and needed. I had to make sure they understood that we were here, and we were growing as we were going through this together. I quickly made a Facebook group called Kahlena Moves Online. People could join us for classes run through Facebook Live, or they could watch the video after the fact whenever it fit into their new schedule by purchasing a one month trial or one year membership. For those who did not use Facebook – which is a surprisingly large number of people – I figured out how to keep them engaged through Zoom. Many of our usual classes could not be done virtually as they use equipment people do not have at home, so my teaching staff went from thirteen down to three of us who consistently taught throughout the pandemic lockdown.

Once I had the group set up, I added the clients I was friends with on Facebook. I then texted, emailed, and Facebook messaged all my clients and invited them to join our new online group where we would be doing live classes. Thankfully, people were very supportive, and most embraced this new format; they wanted to keep moving just as much as we did.

Shifting to teaching online has been both fun and challenging. I've had to learn how to project music properly, how to create the best set up in the studio or in our homes, and how to navigate having our families around during classes – it makes for an interesting class when your four-year-old sneaks out of her room unannounced and jumps on your back to scare you while you're demonstrating child's pose. It has been a humbling experience, and it has taught both the teachers and the clients to be more patient and understanding with one another, especially when unexpected circumstances arise.

There have also been some benefits to this new format. Our clients have been able to take classes they normally wouldn't be able to attend because of their schedules or other life commitments. They have enjoyed getting to know us teachers on a more personal level as we all have more time to connect over Zoom without having to rush off to work or another class. I also decided to use the gaps in our schedule due to the classes that can't be done at home to try out some new formats and styles. It was fun to create these classes for our regulars and get their feedback, and we will be adding them to our schedule as we return to the studio.

Another benefit of moving online and reducing our class schedule is that I was given some much-needed time with my family. It was wonderful to be home with my daughter, husband, and dog and enjoy regular walks, talks, playtime, cleaning, cooking, and other things I don't always have time to do. With that being said, I am a social being, and before long the isolation was starting to get to me. My husband has not worked in three years due to anxiety, depression, PTSD, and obsessive rumination disorder. This means I am the sole provider, and much of this income comes from my studio as well as teaching classes at other locations. It is hard to get away from home other than to work because my husband can only do so much on a daily basis; he's an amazing dad and husband, but his anxiety kicks in and I have to come back. So, my work is also my social time. Now that I was home A LOT, this whole situation was almost harder. My husband also struggled – he wasn't used to having all of us home all the time to watch his daily routine of obsessive cleaning and tidying. It was a big adjustment for all of us.

While I did my best to rest and spend time with my family, I knew I needed to start building the next pieces of my business. We had no idea how long this pandemic was going to last, so I needed to plan for the long-term just in case. After getting a glimpse of the isolation my husband goes through on a regular basis, I realized how many people were cut off from the world around them due to anxiety, mental health issues, or physical ailments. This quickly led to me wanting to give back to those who are isolated and need some support.

I started dancing outside Amica Seniors Living Residence in North Vancouver, located across the street from my studio, with a few ladies who had already been going twice a week. The residents were directed to come out on their balconies, and we led them through some light stretching, movement, and dancing. I got so much enjoyment out of this experience that I soon asked Amica if I could do the other three days a week with the help of some of my clients and friends, and they agreed.

Next, I decided to spread this support to the Ever Green House next to Lions Gate Hospital in North Vancouver. We danced outside the building in honour of International Dance Day, and we then headed to the ER for the 7:00 p.m. cheer to show our support for LGH and all of their essential workers, flash mob style. It was pouring rain the whole way through, but the show must go on!

This was the beginning of the Kahlena Curbside Crew – six to seven clients and friends who volunteer their time to come dance with me and spread love, joy, hope, and movement to those who can't get out on their own, those who just need their day brightened, and those who are in need of some light in the dark days of this pandemic. We have really enjoyed being able to give back to our community in such a unique way, and we are grateful to be able to move our bodies and inspire others to move theirs. The residents of these buildings come outside with walkers, wheelchairs, or canes to participate however they can – even if that means just sitting on a bench, listening to the music, and enjoying some human interaction – and it has been great to see some of them become more mobile over the past seven months.

These interactions have also been a much-needed addition to my own daily routine. Knowing that I am providing something positive for these people in our community has been a light for me, and it has been an honour to be a source of certainty in such uncertain times.

The Kahlena Curbside Crew continues to spread joy and a love of dance throughout the Lower Mainland. We were invited back to Lions Gate for Nurses Week in May as well as to their fundraising week in July, and we will be collaborating on a video project with Lions Gate Hospital Foundation in the near future. We were also invited by BG Homes in Vancouver to lead an eight-week movement series for their senior residents. We were asked to dance for Mother's Day for client's moms on their patios from a distance, and we even got to do an outdoor Summer Series at Lonsdale Quay which we called Dancing On The Deck. We will continue on until the weather changes, and then we will revisit how we can keep these residents moving through the winter months. I am happy to dance in the rain and snow, but it is perhaps not as good for those with mobility issues. We will have to shift indoors somehow, and we will be examining that process as we see the new protocols and numbers.

While I've enjoyed exploring the opportunities that have been presented to me, my pandemic experience hasn't been all sunshine and roses. I had to negotiate a new lease with my landlord during the shutdowns, and there were times when I thought I would have to close my doors and pack it in because things were going so poorly. I had to learn to have difficult conversations with her, negotiate in the face of an uncertain future, and find a way for us to work together. It was a huge learning experience for me as a business owner, and what kept me going – both during these negotiations and through the pandemic as a whole – was maintaining a positive outlook. So, to finish off this chapter, I would like to share with you some of the mantras that help me get through tough times, my daily routine, and life. Repeat these every day to help shift your mindset so that you can keep moving towards your goals.

- Love yourself, others, and every situation – no matter what the outcome may be.
- My body is always working toward optimum health. My body wants to be whole and healthy. I cooperate and become healthy, whole and complete.
- The unexpected and incredible belong to this world. Only then is life made whole.

There is still uncertainty as we look to what the future will bring and how the rest of this pandemic will play out. However, I refuse to let that hold me back. I will keep pushing forward with positivity and persistence, just like I have always done, so

I can pursue my passions. I will continue to provide my clients with opportunities to move their bodies and connect with others. And I will keep bringing energy, love, and kindness into this world, using whatever tools I have at my disposal. My vision has not faded; it is still there, bright as ever, and it will always guide my way.

About Karen Kobel

Karen Kobel is a performer, instructor of dance, yoga and Pilates, and founder of Kahlena Movement Studio. With a BFA in Dance Performance from East Carolina University, she has been dancing for thirty-eight years and teaching for the past twenty-five. She has had the opportunity to perform with Mia Michaels, Jay Norman, Lynn Simonson, Marjon Van Grunsven, Katiti King, Tomi Galaska, Peter Grey Terhune Presents, Princess Cruises, and many local dance collectives.

Karen has also been teaching Pilates for seventeen years. Combining Simonson Dance Technique with Pilates and CI training, Karen has created a unique class format that not only allows the body to flow from movement to movement, but also allows the mind to connect to the present moment, leaving her clients feeling rejuvenated, renewed, and restored.

After returning from Kenya and Uganda in November 2013, where she taught HIV women Pilates, dance and strength training and listened to their life stories, she realized her life purpose was to inspire others – especially women – to find their own voice just as she did after focusing on finding hers. Karen shares her experiences with others in the hopes that it will help them believe that anything and everything is possible!

www.kahlena.com
Email: info@kahlena.com
Facebook: Kahlena Movement Studio
Instagram: @kahlenamovement
Twitter: @kahlenamovement

13

The Gift of Slowing Down

by Jennifer Nagel

"There is a vitality, a life force, an energy, a quickening that is translated through you into action, and because there is only one of you in all of time, this expression is unique. And if you block it, it will never exist through any other medium and it will be lost. The world will not have it. It is not your business to determine how good it is nor how valuable nor how it compares with other expressions. It is your business to keep it yours clearly and directly, to keep the channel open."
Martha Graham

The Gift of Slowing Down

By Jennifer Nagel

My suitcases were all packed and ready to go for my flight the next day when everything came to an abrupt halt. Travel plans were cancelled, workshops were postponed, and client meetings could no longer happen in person. Waves of emotions came along – overwhelm, disbelief, sadness, frustration, and confusion – as we waded through the chaos of navigating work, school, and life in this new reality. I remember the stress and anxiety of figuring out online school for each of my kids while my husband and I both sorted out working from home and we all adjusted to being under the same roof, all day, every day.

Yes, we were all facing this global pandemic together, yet we also had our own unique challenges to deal with. As a therapist, workshop facilitator, and leader of experiential personal and professional growth programs, so much of my work involved face-to-face interaction. Once the pandemic hit, I was confronted with the question of what this would mean for me as well as the financial impact of cancelling the many programs planned for this year, both locally and overseas. Knowing that chaos is essential for change, I literally and figuratively took a breath, shifting my initial panic into a resolve and determination to figure out what I needed to do and how I needed to be for my sense of self and my family. I had to find a way to continue living out my purpose and passion.

Seeing people online wasn't brand new for me as I had already been having sessions with a few clients and supervising therapists from different parts of the world through this format, although the majority of my work was up close and personal. However, teaching online programs to groups was something I had never even considered doing before the pandemic. In fact, if you had told me a year ago that I would be teaching experiential programs online, I likely would have laughed it off. How could you have the depth of connection and transformational work that happens in live workshops through a virtual format? But a global pandemic really brings everything to a pause – a literal standstill – giving you space to reconsider and make the best out of what might be possible. I converted a small storage room inside my garage back into the office it was originally intended to be as it was far enough from the main area of the house to allow for privacy and confidentiality. Little did I realize that this small room with a window looking out into the backyard would become the hub for my international work!

In May 2020, I was invited by an organization in Wuhan – where the coronavirus originated – to present an online program for the people of China about the impacts of the strict quarantine on family relationships. People had been in a lockdown for seventy-six days, and isolation has a way of heightening issues that may have already been present but were kept under the surface or hidden by the normal, everyday act of keeping busy. Many people were experiencing anxiety, depression, anger, and fear. Here was an opportunity for them to come together in an online community, gain awareness about and give voice to their inner experience, and realize that although they had been in isolation, there was this collective community of experience happening. The realization that maybe they were not so alone in this also allowed them to go on a journey of discovering their own wisdom, intuition, and creativity in responding to the stressful situations around them.

At the end of the six weeks, the feedback from the participants was that they felt more connected, were more self-aware, and had more compassion for themselves and others while also experiencing more joy and hope. Many shared that they had learned to connect better within themselves, which then allowed them to connect better with others and with life in general. What I have learned and continue to learn in the work I do globally is that there are some universal aspects to all human beings no matter what their country, culture, religion, socio-economic status, or family history. When we get underneath all the differences in the ways people cope and survive under stress, the deeper yearnings are all the same: connection, belonging, love, safety, freedom, and peace.

I had been having my own doubts and fears about my ability to deliver any kind of quality program online, but the experience of connecting with this group was a gift that proved to me what could be possible! I had to adapt the way I approached the program, which meant learning how to effectively utilize online platforms and maximize participant involvement and interaction. I found that leading guided meditations at the beginning of each session was a wonderful way to bring everyone together energetically and to connect participants with themselves and each other, facilitating a sense of safety and creating an openness to learning and growth. The importance of developing creative visuals for slides became clear as well as finding effective ways to use breakout rooms for dyad practice and small group discussions. I soon learned that as long as the technology was working smoothly, I could still experience an energetic connection and vitality with people. And yes, there were some moments of stress and frustration when the technology was NOT working smoothly, but there was also the opportunity to practice acceptance of whatever was happening in the moment, staying present, re-centering myself, and being able to go with the flow a little more. What a beautiful experience it was to hold space for a group of participants who were physically scattered yet were able to come together as a group in a shared online space. Allowing myself to stretch and shift my beliefs about what was possible in the midst of physical and geographical limitations opened me up to experiencing more grace, forgiveness, and humour within myself.

Meanwhile, a colleague from the other side of the US and I began co-hosting Zoom support calls for therapists and people in helping professions who were connected with the non-profit organizations we do some training programs for – professionals from the US, Canada, Thailand, Malaysia, Singapore, China, Israel, India, and Kenya were joining these calls. We met weekly for the first few months of the pandemic and continue to meet monthly now, coming together to share a reading or poem, lead a guided meditation, and discuss a topic related to transformational change and current happenings around the world. Coming together in community, connection, love, and acceptance. Bringing people together who would never have otherwise met and experiencing a sense of community and connection with one another has been a profound gift. I learned that one does not need to travel overseas and change time zones in order to spread love and acceptance around the world. I have also learned that this energy of love and acceptance travels across the ether, through computer screens, and translates into all languages.

The learning that has come from this pandemic has extended outside of my professional life. When I pause to think about how this virus has impacted me and shifted my perspective, the first part that comes to mind is the slowing down that came with it. For years I had been saying "I need to slow down," to the point that it had become somewhat of a joke with close friends and colleagues who would smile in disbelief at the thought that I would ever actually act on it. I had been constantly on the move even when not travelling overseas, running from meetings to clients to curriculum planning to leading workshops to kids' activities and school pick-ups and homework assistance and dinner preparation and on and on.

When the world came to a standstill, there were moments of panic and anxiety, but there were also some beautiful opportunities for deeper self-care. Going for walks in the forest became an act of mindful meditation. Working from home gave me the opportunity to actually BE at home – no hurried commutes to the office in the morning or rushing from one activity to the next. In their place were new rhythms of slowing down, pausing, and remembering to breathe. Even the act of shopping for groceries became an exercise in taking my time and being intentional about what food to choose from the nearly empty shelves.

What we choose to focus on impacts our whole experience. If we choose to focus on the frustration of everything taking longer or the angst of an unpredictable future, then we end up feeding the energy of frustration and fear. And where does that get us? Instead, we can choose to use this time as an opportunity to be open to new possibilities. This is where chaos comes in. Whenever a foreign element comes along to shake up the old status quo, we go into a period of chaos where the old way no longer fits and we are not clear what else is possible. The gift in this is that we have an opportunity to dig deep and connect with our resourcefulness — our creativity, caring, and wisdom.

Each of us have all the resources we need for healing and growth within us, and the gift in slowing down is that we can make time to seek answers from within as we navigate what is going on around us. Take the time to pause and reconnect with what stirs your soul and gives you a sense of purpose. Allow yourself to sit with the question of, "How can I move through this period of uncertainty with grace, wisdom, and creativity so I can continue serving my purpose?" This might mean setting out on a whole new trajectory and discovering a world of possibility that would have previously been completely unexplored were it not for the chaos of being thrown into the unknown. The essential part is to reconnect, revitalize, and remind yourself of your passion and purpose. For myself, I found that walking amongst the trees and along the beach allowed space for meditating and praying about my various questions around the uncertainty I was experiencing. The answers would present themselves in various forms such as thoughts, feelings, sensations, or whispers of intuition. Being open to and curious about these answers allowed for opportunities to unfold and offered me the choice to step into the uncertainty by taking action.

Another aspect that helped me to shift my perspective was to move away from "what if" and toward "what is." Rather than asking what would happen if I was never able to work in the same way again, I shifted to asking, "At this moment I am unable to meet in large groups or travel anywhere outside of Canada. What IS possible for me to do within these limitations?" We do not necessarily need to *like* the way things are at the moment, but we can work on *accepting* them. With acceptance comes a freedom to then focus our energy on what might be possible rather than using our energy to worry, panic, or shut down completely. For myself, I asked what it might mean to create new programs online and what technology I would need to learn to do this. How could I transform my business in a way that would work during this season of physical distancing, and then go about finding people (colleagues, friends, or experts who I could learn from) who might be able to support me in making these possibilities a reality?

As we saw with our group in China, slowing down also has a way of bringing to light and heightening whatever relationship challenges existed pre-pandemic. This also became evident in my private practice work with individuals, couples, and families as many decided to take this opportunity to face the issues that they had been burying, ignoring, or setting aside in order to just get through the daily tasks of living. There seemed to be an overall heightening of anxiety, depression, stress, and loneliness brought about by the conditions of quarantine and physical distancing. The gift in bringing challenges to the surface and naming them is that you can then choose to put time and energy into working through them — as difficult and painful as it might be — so you can come to a place of new opportunities for healing and growth.

Slowing down has allowed me to have a deeper connection with my family as well. Being around for my children more has allowed me to face the issues I could once temporarily run away from by flying off to teach somewhere, and being confronted with the need to work through things in my own personal life instead of avoiding them has been such a blessing for me. As much as I love to travel the world and experience the personal connections I make through my work, I am learning to appreciate the grounded, centered presence of being in the same time zone for an extended period of time. In spite of continuing to be very busy with online programs and my private practice, I am feeling more rested and grounded on a deeper level. What I am realizing is that I can continue to work from a greater energy of rest once this pandemic has passed. This is another blessing that I may have missed entirely if it were not for the world coming to a standstill.

This slowing down and being grounded is not only a potential gift for the individual, but also for the entire planet. The Earth is certainly grateful for the reprieve from all the pollution in the air. There are blue skies in places that had seldom seen such vibrant colours, birds singing in abundance, and a calm stillness that I experience as being peaceful and connected with the bigger picture of what truly matters. In a world where there is so much chaos and conflict happening amongst people, politics, religions, and hierarchies, perhaps it is essential now more than ever that we intentionally turn to nature to reconnect, recharge, and restore. Being in nature and remembering to pause, breathe, and notice the beauty in the world can remind us to listen to the wisdom in slowing down. Through this, we can remember that there are infinite possibilities, even within our current limitations, when we are open to them.

About Jennifer Nagel

Jennifer Nagel is a clinical counsellor who works with individuals, couples, and families of all ages and is the author of *Magic in the Muck: Finding Grace in Chaos*. She is also a contributing author for the fourth WOW Woman Of Worth bestselling book, Moms in Business: Success Stories with Soul. She travels the world and teaches professional and personal growth programs in countries such as Canada, China, and Kenya, along with providing clinical supervision for other therapists. She has worked with diverse groups including therapists, social workers, educators, school programs, community groups, at-risk youth, non-profit organizations, and corporate groups.

Jennifer is also very involved with the Satir Institute of the Pacific, a non-profit organization that provides programs for personal and professional growth and transformation.

She has spent the past twenty years learning, studying, and applying the Satir Model (based on the work and teachings of family therapy pioneer Virginia Satir) in facilitating transformational change work. Jennifer is passionate about teaching and mentoring others in the use of Satir Transformational Systemic Therapy and helping others to reconnect with the magic of who they truly are.

Jennifer lives in Surrey, BC, Canada with her husband, Rod, and their children, Mahalia and Kai.

www.jennifernagelcounselling.com
www.magicinthemuck.com
Facebook: @jennifernagelcounselling
LinkedIn: Jennifer Nagel

14

Unsinkable

by Sam van Born

"Be safe, stay healthy, and reach out if you need anything – I'm here to help you"
Sam van Born

Unsinkable

By Sam van Born

When 2020 arrived, I was feeling great. It was a new year, a new decade, one where everything was going to change. I was confident in my business, and the rollercoaster of recovering from an abusive relationship was once again on a downswing. There was some news about this flu-like sickness going on, but it was just the flu. How bad could it be? And then March arrived, and everything changed – not just for me but for the entire world. A global pandemic found its way into my life, and as a single mother, a first responder, and a businesswoman, I wasn't sure how I was going to make it through. I thought juggling our life was challenging in the past; I didn't realize how hard it was going to get.

I was off on vacation at the time, having booked twenty days off around spring break. I had scheduled a babysitting course and an art camp for my daughter, and then we were going to just spend time together and not have to worry about or focus on work or school. Unfortunately, a number of guys from the fire hall were off travelling, and as the pandemic crept closer and closer, management realized they needed extra bodies at the hall to cover everyone's self-isolation periods. I was asked to come back to work and defer a set of my holidays, and since there was not a lot going on, I obliged.

During my first shift back, we were asked to clean, clean, clean. Training was set aside, along with our normal daily activities that I had been used to doing for the last twenty years. Then, to help reduce the risk of spreading the virus, we were assigned to a group of four who stayed on the same truck for the entirety of two days and two nights. We were told to separate into different rooms with no more than two people cooking meals, to sanitize surfaces, and to wash our hands diligently. When we went out on a call, my job as the captain was to keep an eye on who touched what and do assessments from the doorway to screen people for symptoms and identify those who might have been recently exposed. We were focused on keeping ourselves safe so that we didn't bring anything back to the hall, or to our families.

The first couple of calls I was sent on went pretty smoothly, but by the end of the day I could tell that panic had set in. People were scared and needed reassurance from us as first responders that we were there to help them. As a result, they often didn't tell us the full scope of what they were feeling or why we were there to help them. People were to report flu-like symptoms to the dispatcher, so we could don extra protective equipment to keep ourselves safe. Instead, we would walk into a call and find people sitting there with masks on, only to learn they were waiting for their test results. In some cases, they would even go to the extent of not disclosing fevers and coughs. We tried our best to stay calm, be professional, and support the public through the mass hysteria that was surrounding us. But by the end of my shift – at which point we were setting up a triage centre in the parking lot of the local hospital – things were getting real and I was getting scared.

Throughout my shift, my eighty-three-year-old mum, who had previously battled lung cancer, kept my eleven-year-old daughter company during the day while a nanny stayed with her overnight. When I came home from that first shift, I realized I couldn't hug or kiss my mum because I didn't know whether I'd been exposed, and the last thing I wanted was for her to get sick and possibly die alone. I broke down in tears as the stress of the day and all the information that was flooding in got to me.

I quickly decided that my mother could no longer watch my daughter for her own safety. Unfortunately, my nanny also informed me that she would no longer be able to come and stay at my place – she needed to keep her family and the other family she was working for safe – and that the next two nights would be the last for now. I started to panic. I had no one to look after my child, yet I still needed to work. There was childcare available for first responders, but at this time it was only available from nine to five, Monday to Friday, which didn't work with my shifts. And in the back of my mind, I wondered if I really wanted my daughter spending a bunch of time with other kids she didn't know outside the safety of our home. What would that even look like? I felt completely alone and had no idea what I was going to do, and I only had twelve days of holiday left to figure it out.

Fortunately, I spoke to a neighbour that I had become friends with over the last year, and I learned she also was a little worried about going in and out of stores and needed childcare for her work as a sales rep. So, the two of us decided to band together and help each other out. From that day forward, each of our kids knew that they could go back and forth between our two houses. Our bubbles were extremely small – it was just the four of us, and the two of us going to work.

Over the next few weeks, I got lost in the updates and news. I watched as the hospitals in Italy and New York surpassed capacity and ran out of ventilators. I read articles on first responders being forced to reuse their masks due to a worldwide shortage. It was relentless, and it felt almost like mass hysteria. Eventually, I realized this was not good for my mental health and decided to take what I knew and the updates I was being given through work and use that information to keep my loved ones safe. No more news, no more going down the rabbit hole of never-ending statistics and theories. I was maxed out. At this point, all I could focus on was going to work, finding the food that we needed, and getting enough so I wasn't going to the store every other day while making sure to leave enough for others. I got some help from a local mum group to pick up a small stand-up freezer from my mum's house and deliver it to my place so I could store a few extra things.

The first few weeks of the shutdowns were really hard. The babysitting course that my daughter was supposed to take, which she was extremely excited about, was cancelled. Her art class was also cancelled. Then spring break ended but she could not return to school. Life as a preteen is hard enough, but now her whole world had been turned upside down. It was difficult to navigate all of these changes as an adult; I can't imagine being eleven and having to go through this.

During this time, my business went on the back burner. I am a social business partner for Alovéa, which is a company that provides whole food plant-based nutritional products that focus on helping people bolster their immune systems, lower inflammation, and support their hormones, along with an award-winning hemp/CBD oil. While these products have a lot of benefits in the midst of a global pandemic – especially the ones that support a strong immune system – with all the uncertainty around me, people losing their jobs, and stores shutting down, sharing information about them wasn't in the forefront of my mind. I did stock up on products for my daughter and I just in case the postal service got shut down or production stopped. Thankfully, I soon found out that there was no threat of being shut down because our manufacturing plant supported FEMA, and although delivery through the postal service was slow, we were still able to receive products.

In April, online learning became our new reality. My daughter had class every day, and the extreme frustration and isolation that came with it often had her in tears. At first the Grade Sixes and Sevens were combined, but it quickly became apparent that the two grades needed to be split. There were too many kids on the platform, and one group would have to sit and wait quietly while the other was being addressed. Her teacher was very organized and seemed to have the system down pat, but the kids did not have the attention span to focus on a video call for an hour every day. My daughter missed the independence she felt walking to and from school on her own and the connections she gained from being amongst her peers. On my end, it was extremely frustrating and hard to set her up on different platforms with old technology. At first we thought setting up kid's messenger to allow her to communicate with her friends, but everyone decided to iMessage instead. So, I had to make the switch from Android to Apple – it was confusing at first, but I figured it out.

Then June came and brought with it the option to return to in-person classes, which had its own set of challenges and concerns. Do you send your child back to school, or do you continue with online learning? My daughter was able to go back full-time because I'm a first responder, and we decided to go for it. I knew she would benefit greatly from physically going to class, and I trusted the school and the teachers to do everything they could to keep her safe. I did my best to explain to her that it was going to be different, probably a lot stricter, and to keep an open mind. Thankfully, she thrived.

Thirty days later, it was summer. By this time the situation had caused so much anxiety that as she was heading to bed one night, my daughter told me she was having troubles breathing. My thoughts immediately went to the worst-case scenario. I called work and told them I couldn't come in for my shift the next day, then spent two hours on hold on the nurses' line to go through her signs and symptoms. They told me it sounded like she had anxiety, and I agreed with their assessment. The next night, the two of us went out to kick a soccer ball around. She didn't get winded, so I knew she was okay.

Because I had deferred a set of holidays, I was able to have almost the entire month of July off. We were able to do some small local vacations during this time, and it was good to get away. We slowly started to increase our bubble but still kept it small. My daughter enjoyed going to the local field where other families would bring their dogs to run around. These dogs made her extremely happy, and for months we would go there every single night to get some more unconditional love.

Things were starting to turn around, but I was still feeling extremely unmotivated and all my feelings were heightened. Then, one of my friends sent me a link to a documentary/movie called *Unsinkable* about the law of attraction and how negative thoughts bring more negativity into your life. One of the quotes really stuck with me: "I don't know why this is happening, but one thing I know for sure: something big, something huge, something way bigger than me will come out of this, because I am not going through all this for nothing!" This was the kick I needed, to reset – to move forward in my business and just life in general. I was forty-eight, perimenopausal, had gained twenty pounds, and was living in the middle of a pandemic. Something needed to shift. Like many people, what was holding me back was – and to be honest, still is – my thoughts. I've lost myself over the last few decades, and now I do way too much for others and not enough for myself. I don't even know what I enjoy anymore, which makes it hard to find the motivation to do something for myself. I'm feeling stuck in the negativity that surrounds me and I haven't quite yet figured out how to break the cycle. But what I do know is that mindset is everything; if you change the way you think, you change the way you feel.

My business has certainly helped me focus on the good things happening in the world. Alovéa is all about giving hope to others. We are on a mission to give 100+ million servings of nutritional support to children in need with our Buy 1, Nourish 2™ giving model – for every serving of Alovéa's integrated health products that is purchased, we donate a serving to children in need. We are collaborating with Operation Underground Railroad with the intention of donating tens of thousands of meals to their aftercare centres in both Uganda and Ghana, each of which is caring for 500-600 children that have been rescued from the child sex trafficking industry. Dr. Renee Hirte from A Dream for the Cure Cancer Research Foundation is using our Acemannan products (a stabilized, concentrated form of aloe vera) and our award-winning hemp

CBD oil in her clinical trials and research in immunotherapy for brain cancer patients at the Mayo clinic, and there is also a clinical trial starting in Nigeria to support people with sickle cell disease. These are huge goals, and they prompted me to get my own goals back on track. With us expanding globally, I feel motivated now more than ever to help people all over the world.

With this new norm of dealing with a deadly global pandemic, it is imperative that I am able to keep the virus at bay, not only by taking extra precautions at work but also through my business. I wholeheartedly believe that if you give your body what it needs, it will do what it was designed to do: HEAL itself. With the return to school just around the corner, I am focusing on helping families who are sending their kids back to school – along with others who would benefit from these products – to support and strengthen their immune systems.

With so many people losing their jobs and the uncertainty we are all facing, the biggest lesson I have learned is to try your best to keep positive, lean on those close to you, be kind, and stay present. There is so much conflicting information, conspiracy theories, and fear-mongering that it is hard to know what's true and what's not. We are having to make decisions to protect ourselves and our families, and there should not be any shame or blame toward others that choose differently than you. That old saying of you never know what others are going through really rings true; everyone has a story, and you never know where someone is in theirs. So let's focus on the good, support our friends and families, and bring more positivity into our lives – in this way, we become unsinkable.

About Sam van Born

Sam van Born was born and raised in North Vancouver, BC where she lives with her almost twelve-year-old daughter. She wasn't sure exactly what she wanted to do in life until she had a conversation with her friend's dad who was a captain in the fire service. Inspired to find out more about this amazing career, she soon moved out to Lions Bay to join the volunteer fire department. A year later she got into a firefighting school in Alberta, and eleven weeks after that she was certified. She was then hired by the North Vancouver City Fire Department, and now, almost twenty-one years later, she has worked her way through the ranks to become a full-time captain.

Sam is also actively promoting health and wellness through her home-based business with Alovéa, which was founded by two international not-for-profit organizations. This company provides sustainable solutions to the world's most challenging health concerns in the form of nutraceutical products that focus on strengthening people's immune systems, antioxidants, inflammation, hormone support, along with an award-winning Hemp/CBD Oil. With the company expanding globally, she'll be busy helping a lot of people around the world.

Website: samvanborn.myalovea.com
facebook.com/samvanborn.myalovea/
facebook.com/groups
aloveaoperationundergroundrailroad/
Email: sammyvan89@gmail.com
Instagram: @samvanborn
LinkedIn: Sam Van Born

15

Chaotic Stillness in the Eye of the Storm

by Cathy Derksen

*"Life isn't about waiting for the storm to pass.
It's about learning how to dance in the rain."*
Vivian Greene

Chaotic Stillness in the Eye of the Storm

By Cathy Derksen

Without warning, the storm hit. The rain pounded down, falling so hard, so violently, that it ricocheted back up off the ground. The wind rushed past me, and with it debris of all sizes that whipped past my face. The whole community was in a panic, not knowing what had hit us or when it would end. Everyone kept asking me what to do. They looked to me for leadership and pressed me as if I was their lifeboat keeping them above water. How was I supposed to help all these people? Did they think I was superwoman? I was exhausted and overwhelmed in my own state of panic, doing my best to protect and support my family.

The pandemic had arrived, and my world had been thrown into chaos.

For most people, the shutdowns brought about a time of isolation in which daily activities stopped and life came to a standstill. For me, it was the opposite. My position as a financial planner turned into a type of emergency response role. I have over 250 people who depend on me to give them guidance and support on every aspect of their financial life, and as the economy came crashing to a halt, they all turned to me, desperately hoping I could help them escape from the panic and chaos. I was their sounding board as they tried to make sense of their life savings disappearing before their eyes. I was their last resort as they looked for assurance that they wouldn't be losing their homes, even though their jobs were gone indefinitely and they had no way to pay their bills. Businesses that had been booming only weeks earlier were closing their doors with no way to pay their employees or the bills they already had on the books.

It wasn't just their financial worries that they shared with me. They were anxious about family members being cut off from each other and people becoming hospitalized, unable to have any physical contact with their loved ones, and they needed to let out these thoughts that were overwhelming them. Panic had set in on many levels, and I was holding my community on my shoulders.

As the storm swirled around me, the trauma pushed me into a place of chaotic stillness. In the eye of the storm, I clung to a tree for support and caught my breath. It was this moment of stillness that allowed me the clarity to reflect on my situation and see that my current job was not feeding my need to be of service and help other people create success – it was draining my energy and leaving me exhausted and frustrated.

Years ago, I chose a career in financial planning as a way of helping others improve their lives. I saw that many people had financial challenges that impacted many other aspects of their life, and I wanted to help turn this around. But as I began to realize how the day-to-day processes of my work were sapping my energy, I also saw that I was not having the positive impact that I thought I would. My passion for helping others hadn't changed, but I wanted to shift my approach to bring more value to my community. I needed to be of service in a way that would bring me joy and inspiration instead of draining me. I needed to be of service in a way that would bring lasting change to the lives I touched. I came to the realization that I will continue to provide financial planning services, but will also add a level of support that brings me joy and is valuable to my community.

My ability to be a source of support for my family and my community of clients and friends during these turbulent times has been greatly bolstered by the personal development programs I had been working on before this virus changed our lives. These programs provided me with a supportive community of positive people who were focused on creating strategies for success rather than dwelling on the potential negative impact of the pandemic, and they have been my primary source of inspiration to shift my focus.

As the summer arrived and the storm began to subside, I had more time to work on my passion project: an online community focused on helping women follow their dreams and step into a life that brings them joy. I had begun this project earlier in the year as a way to broaden my social circle and support women in the community, but the onset of the pandemic and the stress it brought added another level of determination for me to expand my reach. My big goal is to create a cycle of success and wealth among women—as women create success in their life, they often help others do the same. Through the lessons I learned in those personal development programs, I am able to lead my community in discovering what brings them joy and learning how to move forward to reach their goals. We meet regularly on Zoom and Facebook Live to share our challenges and triumphs. I present material on success strategies and we discuss books and events we have enjoyed. I also have one-on-one calls with members of the community to help them dig deeper into their personal development.

Many people found themselves in the same place I was at the beginning of this pandemic: realizing that they were unhappy with their current situation and renewing their interest in passions that had been forgotten or set aside. However, when it comes to committing to following a new path, many of us are afraid to take the leap. We fear what other people will think. We fear the possibility of failure. We fear the discomfort we may have to endure to make changes in our life. It is critical to keep yourself focused on your goals and to push through the fear to find success. In order to do this, you need to ask yourself: do you want to spend the rest of your life just filling time with day-to-day activities, or do you want to have a purpose in your life that brings you joy and contributes to the world?

When you feel that life is drifting past you, its time to take a leap of faith and create a life that brings you joy. Allow yourself to shine! Give yourself permission to think about yourself and where you want the next chapter of your life to lead. Will you go back to school? Start a new business? Discover new hobbies? Spend more time with friends? Travel the world? Whatever it may be, find the support you need to take those next steps forward and embrace your passion and purpose.

For example, one member of my community had been feeling stuck and frustrated for many years. She had a great job, her marriage was solid, and her kids were in university, so she felt she should be happy with her life. She felt guilty about her desire for more fulfilment. After joining my community and allowing herself to reflect on her own goals and dreams, she found the motivation to pursue her love of fitness that she had let go of because she was "too old" and "didn't have time." Now she is feeling energized and excited about life again – she simply had to get the spark of inspiration and then receive support, encouragement, and tools to move forward from the community.

Another member had dedicated her life to climbing the ladder in the law firm she worked for. She was a partner in the business and had all the material things we associate with success: a beautiful home, fancy cars, and hired help to look after her needs. Despite all this, she felt something was missing. She felt a calling to leave everything behind and create her own business as a tour guide. By spending time in the online community and learning new skills to challenge and change the beliefs that held her back, she has been able to push past her fears of what everyone else would say and stand strong in her decision. Despite the travel restrictions brought on by the pandemic, she has started organizing some trips with great success.

There are many steps to take and lessons to learn as we move forward in creating our own version of success. In the first step, you must allow yourself to envision what you want in your life – not just the general things that you expect to get, but the big-picture things on your bucket list. As women, we often lose track of our own goals as we get busy in our roles as mothers, caretakers, dedicated employees, and business owners. Allow yourself to dream again! Pay attention to what brings you joy; these are the things that will bring your life to life. Your goal should be something that scares you a little – the excitement it creates will help you to stay motivated toward success.

When you have an idea in your mind of what you really want in your life, the next step is to visualize it in great detail and allow yourself to feel the way you would feel if you achieved that goal. This helps your brain to believe that you are able to succeed.

Next, set a date that you plan to complete it by. This helps your subconscious accept this new belief and create your new reality. To help solidify the goal in your mind, write it down and read it everyday. Its also a great idea to record yourself reading your goal statement out loud and listen to it daily. This repetition will create an image of this reality in your subconscious mind. It is our deepest-held beliefs that tell us what we are capable of achieving; by convincing our subconscious that our goal has already become a reality, we remove any self-imposed limits that would hold us back. Our conscious mind sets the logical goals, but our subconscious mind is most often the controller of our actions.

Your ability to make solid decisions and stick with the plan is critical to your success. The world's top personal coaches agree that the people who create success in their lives tend to make decisions quickly and stick with those decisions. In contrast, people who struggle with creating success tend to make decisions slowly and change their minds often. We have all had experiences when we know what we needed to be doing to reach our goal but don't take action. For instance, we might want to lose weight but can't stop ourselves from having a big piece of chocolate cake when offered. Or we might be trying to save money for a big holiday with our family, but buying an expensive coffee every day seems more important.

Once you have made a decision, take immediate action. Don't just think about your idea. Don't ask all of your friends and family what they think. Don't put off acting on it to next week. When you have decided what your goals are, you need to immediately take the first step in that direction. This could be as simple as making a call to someone you think can help you or as large as quitting your current job. Your goal may be huge, but so long as you keep taking action toward it, you will eventually succeed. I often find that as soon as I make a decision and start taking steps toward it, the pieces start coming together in amazing ways. For example, when I decided I needed to improve my online communication skills, Facebook posts popped up with the exact tools I was looking for. I also received an unexpected call from a friend who assisted me in learning how to use Zoom and social media more effectively. Your decision puts the wheels in motion that bring about the changes you need.

Sometimes, what holds us back is a fear of failure due to our past performance. Remember that those results were based on the actions you took and the beliefs you had about your abilities at that time. Moving forward, you can replace your negative, limiting beliefs with inspirational thoughts. I love Ralf Waldo Emerson's quote, "We become what we think about all day long." You've probably noticed that you tend to have the same thoughts running through your mind over and over, day after day, and that most of these thoughts are focused on worry and challenge. Imagine what would happen if you replaced these thoughts, which create anxiety and limitations, with thoughts of inspiration and success! You can, and that's where I can help.

It's important to note that most of our actions run by habit. Have you ever driven home from work and realized that you don't remember any details of the trip? You were letting your subconscious mind control your actions with very little conscious awareness of the process. This is how we tend to live our lives. We go through our days barely noticing what we are doing as we can complete most tasks without thinking about them. Weeks blow by, then years, and we can't remember many details about any of it. This is especially true during the chaotic, uncertain times brought about by the pandemic – many people left themselves on autopilot, reacting in a panic to the changes going on around us. In contrast, the people who have chosen to consciously respond to these events have found ways to adjust their responses and adapt to this situation. These are the people who have found success even in these challenging times.

Our habits are built around our current beliefs; as Henry Ford once said, "Whether you think you can, or you think you can't, you're right," We make choices and take actions based on what we believe we are capable of. If you think you are not good at public speaking, you will be stressed and stumble on your words. However, if you tell yourself that you are capable of taking on this challenge, you will step up with more confidence. Learning how to shift the beliefs held in your subconscious mind will allow you to change your actions and get the results you want out of life.

Finally, have faith in yourself. I love the quote by one of my mentors, Bob Proctor: "Both faith and fear demand you believe in something you cannot see. You choose." You must make the conscious choice to hold onto the faith that you can create the situation you want. Trust in your ability to reach your goals, and keep in mind that what we often call failure is simply a challenge that creates a learning experience. The only time you truly fail is when you give up and stop moving forward.

I coined the term "inspired tenacity" to describe the approach needed to move forward with your big goals. You need to be truly inspired, and have the tenacity to persevere toward success no matter what challenges come your way. I have named my community Inspired Tenacity to continually remind us of these important factors. Set your attitude on gratitude for every success and look for the positive in every situation. And remember, having an accountability partner and a supportive community to lean on will make your path to success so much smoother – and more fun!

I am amazed that the chaos of the pandemic led me to create this amazing community. Who would have imagined that something so positive and exciting would come out of such an overwhelming experience? I look forward to every day that I can help another person find new ways to bring their life back to life.

Think about your own situation and the potential you have to create a life that brings you more joy. What's next? You decide!

I dedicate this chapter to all the women who are doing their best to improve the quality of life for themselves, their family, and their community. Together we can lift the world to a more positive reality.

About Cathy Derksen

Cathy is dedicated to improving the lives of the women in her community. She transformed her career from working as a lab technologist into financial planning so that she could focus her energy on helping others in a more direct manner. After digging deeper into her innate drive to be of service, she has added another level to her connection within her community. Cathy now provides online resources to assist women in discovering their deeper calling by adjusting their mindset and focus in order to reach their goals. She will help you clarify your next step and apply courage and inspired tenacity to live the life that brings you joy.

Cathy lives in British Columbia, Canada. She enjoys spending time in nature, travelling, meeting new people, and connecting with her community around the world.

www.inspiredtenacity.com
Email: cathy@inspiredtenacity.com

16

Thriving During Quarantine, Guilt Free

by Gail Thevarge

"When you can't control what's happening, challenge yourself to control the way you respond to what's happening. That's where your power is."
Author Unknown

Thriving During Quarantine, Guilt Free

By Gail Thevarge

When the pandemic first arrived, I got caught in a spiral of fear that prevented me from moving forward. Then I decided to look for a different approach that would not only permit me to exist in this new world, but also to thrive. In no way do I want to downplay the severity of this situation or the losses suffered by so many, and I am deeply sorry for all those who have been negatively affected by this pandemic. My vision is to bring a different, more optimistic perspective to show that although so many things are not possible during these unprecedented times, there is still so much that is obtainable – providing that you are willing to look with an open mind and be grateful for the many blessings that you have.

As an empathic person, I am highly susceptible to the

emotions of those around me, whether I want to be or not. Over the years, I have learned to protect myself and my peace through yoga, meditation, workouts, and other healthy practices. In early March I also embarked on a new healthy eating plan as I had gained more than a little unwanted weight and had been making some less than nutritious food choices. I have found in the past that eating clean not only resets my body but also provides me with clarity and focus. I did not know at the time how beneficial this addition to my health regime would be.

The pandemic arrived mid-March, and with it came the quarantine. At first, I was in disbelief; it was beyond my comprehension that the world could and would just stop. I had thought that the people in power would prevent the economy from grinding to a halt. I had been certain that taking a few steps to keep ourselves safe – washing our hands, not touching our faces, staying six feet apart – would be sufficient to prevent the spread of this virus. I had thought the world would continue as usual after a brief shutdown. I was wrong on all accounts.

In terms of employment, I am incredibly grateful to have a job that can be done from home for which I already had the necessary components in place to keep working. On the rare occasion I needed to go to the office, I was there alone and made the commute alone. It was months before I even shared an elevator with another person. This allowed me to keep working and continue paying the bills. I did my part to keep the economy moving by picking up healthy takeout from restaurants as often as I could and purchasing from small local stores when curbside pickup was available.

Unfortunately, my travel plans did not escape the impacts of this virus. At the beginning of the year, I had planned to attend eight running events – two of them were in the United

States while the rest involved travel within British Columbia. The fees were paid, the accommodations were booked, and my training was underway. I had a vision of adding each of the medals I would be receiving at the finish lines to the medal holder I had purchased during a running event in Las Vegas a few years ago. Then, one by one, these runs were cancelled. These events are the highlight of my year, so I was devastated. Deep down, I knew that continuing to run was the best option for my emotional wellbeing, but I just could not get motivated. What was the point? The more I stayed inside, the harder it was to go outside.

Stuck at home, I quickly found myself lost in the overwhelming amount of news about the pandemic. My initial fears were not about catching the virus, but rather what the panic spreading among the masses could result in. With my empathic traits, this uncertainty could draw me down a rabbit hole of fear. I was watching the news and social media daily, hoping to see the numbers decline or that a cure was found. After a few days of scrolling and watching, I realized that I was wasting time being a spectator instead of claiming the title role in my own life. I was allowing what I was seeing in the news to dictate how I felt. In order to change the direction my life was taking, I made an effort to look at this unprecedented time of "quiet" as a gift. It seemed that there were no expectations or quotas to be filled during quarantine, leaving me time to make some changes that would benefit me even after this pandemic was over. This shift in my mindset provided me with a sense of control over my life at a time when I was unable to take part in the running groups and yoga classes that had offered me peace in the past.

Within two weeks of the start of quarantine, and shortly after my change in perspective, I received an email from a running training group that I had been involved with in the past. Looking back on it, I can see that this was another occurrence of an opportunity appearing at a time when it was most needed, and at a time when I was open to receiving it. The timing was impeccable. This group had been planning to launch a new program to help people train for a specific running event – now that the event was going to be cancelled, the plans were changed. Instead of cancelling the training, they decided to switch to an online platform and offer the program for free. The running event would now be virtual. This was the first business that I observed shifting their approach in order to be able to continue in this new reality, and for me, it was a dream come true. The training program landed in my email inbox, and all I had to do was start. I had nine weeks to complete it, and if I did so within that timeframe, they would send me a medal and a shirt. This was a great option to keep things going, although I would miss the excitement of the large crowds at the live events.

This opportunity was the motivation I needed to get back in motion. Before the pandemic started, I had been thinking about getting up earlier and implementing a healthier morning routine. Typically, I would get out of bed, get ready as fast as I could, and blast out the door. I was always rushed, and I felt anxious every day. With the hour saved from my morning commute, I thought this was a perfect opportunity to try out a new routine as I had time to find out what worked best. I started walking my dog at 5:00 a.m., did my run training, then finished it all off with a fifteen-minute meditation. After starting this new practice, I became more relaxed and had a much better attitude to begin my workday. I also found that training in the morning instead of after work allowed me to get it done before any distractions could disrupt my good intentions.

Next, I needed to find somewhere to do my training. Up until now, I had always done it on the walkway along the lake as I enjoyed being by the water. However, during the few times I had gone to the lake after the quarantine began, it did not seem like there was enough room to socially distance. I needed another option. While contemplating the alternatives, I had the idea to run at a sports field close to my home – with all the sports being cancelled, it was now an incredibly quiet place.

The first day, I noticed the marked 1.2-kilometre gravel track around the fields. I had seen this before when I had visited to watch games, but I had not considered it as an option for my own training as I thought running in a large circuit would be tedious. Even when I first started running there, I saw this place only as an opportunity to continue training and nothing more. However, once I looked at the surroundings with new eyes, I saw that it was quite beautiful. There were streams on two sides of the track along with views of the mountains surrounding the town. By going early in the morning, I could watch the sun rise over the mountains on the other side of the lake. What an amazing way to start the day. This area is a five-minute walk from my house – the perfect distance to get a warmup done on the way there and a great way to cool down at the end of the run.

Just getting back to training improved my frame of mind. It provided some assurance that in spite of everything that was going on, there were still some things I was able to do the way I did before the pandemic.

As I was training for this first event, other virtual running event registrations appeared in my inbox. One event that I had planned to attend with a friend not only switched to a virtual race but also sent out swag bags prior to the event, which included the shirt, some amazing chocolates, and the medal as well as other goodies. I was able to run the event with my friend – socially distanced, of course – which made it more exciting than my usual training runs.

As more virtual events appeared, the online community became larger. People were posting their pictures and results. Trainers were providing advice and offering encouragement. Events that I had been unable to attend pre-COVID due to conflicting schedules or travel costs now became available to me. The Rock 'n' Roll Marathon events that would typically take place at various destinations around the world became free virtual events with medals and shirts available to purchase. I began doing these events most weekends, even doing two events on a weekend known as the Remix Challenge. I was running more and spending less.

The benefits I saw from this change in approach started me looking for other blessings during this unique time. My new training spot is a quiet refuge, except for the numerous birds who nest there. On the days I do not train, I go there to walk and enjoy the peace. People have been painting rocks with kind messages and leaving them beside the path; this small act shows that there are people who care, and that I am not alone. It even seemed to me that the birds were chirping louder during the quarantine – I cannot prove this, but I believe it to be true.

Just prior to the quarantine, I had started two projects. The first, as I mentioned earlier, was to begin a new healthy eating program. Now that I was on track with my run training, the new eating regime seemed like the perfect way to complement it. This program used seasonal produce along with healthy items like quinoa, beans, and brown rice. Even with all the shortages at the grocery stores and the news reports of empty shelves, these items were always available when I looked for them – I did not have the sense of deprivation that seemed to be affecting the masses. Without the temptation of restaurants and social engagements, I found it easier to complete the program and the results were so much better than I had anticipated.

The other project that I had started pre-pandemic was painting the interior of my home, which I had anticipated to be a slow and creative process. I had painted two rooms with the help of a friend, my daughter, and her friends a week before the quarantine began, and I had thought this was a great start. At the time, I figured that I would be able to finish the project within a year. Once everything shut down and I suddenly had more free time, I made it a challenge to complete the work on my own over the course of a couple of weekends. Being able to accomplish this goal felt like a big win and gave me a sense of pride. Also, having a home filled with my own colour choices and furnishings was comforting when so much was out of my control.

To me, things seemed to slow down during quarantine. There was less of everything – less traffic, less noise (except for the birds), less rushing around as there was nowhere to go. I would see posts about people playing games and baking bread, like a scene from simpler times. Siblings who would normally be caught up in their own activities and friends were now spending quality time with each other. Families who once had conflicting schedules were now making and eating meals together.

I implemented some new rituals in my own life during this time. Before, I was always in a rush to get things done; now, I could do everything mindfully. To signal the end of the workday, especially when I was working from home, I began lighting a candle or putting on a diffuser while listening to music that provoked a sense of calm. This is a simple thing that provides me with a sense of relaxation, and I have continued this practice even after returning to the office.

Another way my perspective changed during this time was that I gained a sense of urgency. As so many things that I had taken for granted became unavailable to me, it became clear that nothing is guaranteed. If I have goals and dreams that I want to achieve, I need to start working on them now.

For me, the quiet time I had during quarantine was a gift. I was able to discern what was important to me and what I wanted to accomplish. I do not want to have any regrets about goals not achieved or dreams not fulfilled, and I have been reminded that there is no time to waste. I want every moment to count, and I want to be mindful about all that I do. This does not mean that I must always be on a mission to complete goals, though. I now strive to be fully present in all that I do, and sometimes that includes taking naps or watching the clouds move across the sky.

During difficult times, such as the one we are living through today, it is important to look for opportunities to be grateful. Gratitude can create a positive shift in our own mindset, which ripples out to impact those we are closest to and has the potential to radiate far beyond our own circle of influence. You can be grateful for even the smallest of things: your favourite food is the dinner special at your local restaurant, you have an amazing visit with an old friend, you receive a compliment from a complete stranger. And once you change your mindset, you can change the rest of your life. I hope that I have shown that it is possible to choose a different perspective on living in these turbulent times, and that if we allow ourselves to be open to the changes around us, we can even thrive.

About Gail Thevarge

Gail's mantra is "whatever it takes," and she uses this to complete challenges in all areas of her life. One such challenge came from the restrictions brought about by the pandemic, which forced her to change course and find new ways to continue to stay motivated and live her passions. By sharing her story, she hopes to show a different way to perceive the adversities brought to us all during the uncertain times and to encourage others to seek situations to feel thankful for. Facing new challenges and finding methods to overcome them brings a sense of power and achievement, especially during uncertain times.

Gail's greatest passion is to travel, and she is at her best when she is able to combine runs with travelling to new destinations each year. She resides in Summerland in the beautiful Okanagan Valley and loves spending time with her two amazing children, Taylor and Emily, while awaiting the next big challenge and adventure.

Email: egt_home@shaw.ca
Instagram: @10shalfsandtravel

BECAUSE EVERY WOMAN IS
A WOMAN OF WORTH

Keep Getting WOWed

Join us online for conversations that matter at WOW TV, a free community service where thought leaders, bestselling authors, change agents and celebrities will inspire and empower you:

www.awomanofworth.com/tv

Interested in becoming a contributing author in one of our collaborative bestselling books? Learn more at:

www.awomanofworth.com/become-an-author

"A Taste of WOW" – Your FREE Book is Waiting

This eBook includes eight chapters: one from each book in the original WOW Series, to give you a taste of the powerful and heartfelt writing of our authors. Topics include Moms in Business, Empowered Entrepreneurs, The Power of Collaboration, Life & Leadership with Soul, Aging With Moxie, Mental Health Matters, and Thriving Through Turbulent Times.

Get your free copy of
"A Taste of WOW" here:

www.awomanofworth.com/books

About Woman Of Worth WOW Worldwide

Connect. Collaborate. Celebrate. EMPOWER.
WOW is where empowered women join together to make meaningful connections, collaborate for success, build their businesses, laugh and learn, and celebrate their fabulousness. If you're looking for a place where you can belong, with a group of women who will stand beside you and build you up, then WOW is the place for you. The women who are attracted to WOW are the movers and shakers of the world. They are those who want to make a difference; those who believe in the strength of a community, and those who are wanting and willing to support others, both personally and professionally. We call this "Tribe" and our tribe is amazing. If that sounds like you, take advantage of any of our opportunities and see what all the fuss is about.

www.awomanofworth.com

And be part of our Facebook community at
http://www.facebook.com/aWomanOfWorthWOW